TWELVE PLAYS OF THE NOH AND KYŌGEN THEATERS

D1086889

TWELVE PLAYS OF THE NOH AND KYŌGEN THEATERS

Edited by Karen Brazell

Editorial Assistance by
J. Philip Gabriel

Translators

Monica Bethe
J. Philip Gabriel
Janet Goff
Carolyn Haynes
H. Mack Horton
Eàrl Jackson, Jr.
Eileen Katō
Jeanne Paik Kaufman
Susan Blakeley Klein
Etsuko Terasaki

East Asia Program
Cornell University
Ithaca, New York 14853

The *Cornell East Asia Series* publishes manuscripts on a wide variety of scholarly topics pertaining to East Asia. Manuscripts are published on the basis of camera-ready copy provided by the volume author or editor.

Inquiries should be addressed to Editorial Board, Cornell East Asia Series, East Asia Program, Cornell University, 140 Uris Hall, Ithaca, New York 14853.

ISSN 1050-2955
ISBN 0-939657-00-7

TABLE OF CONTENTS

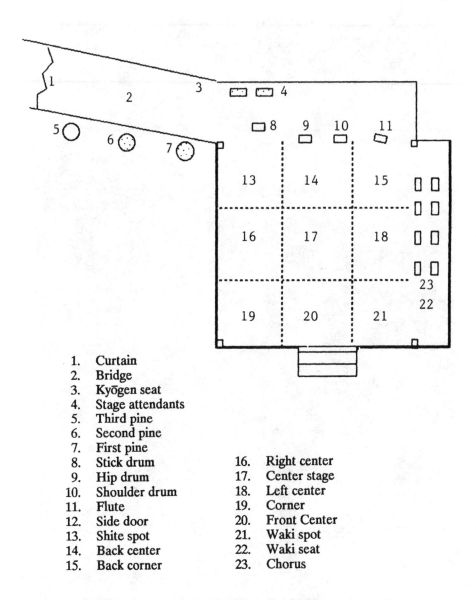

1. Curtain
2. Bridge
3. Kyōgen seat
4. Stage attendants
5. Third pine
6. Second pine
7. First pine
8. Stick drum
9. Hip drum
10. Shoulder drum
11. Flute
12. Side door
13. Shite spot
14. Back center
15. Back corner
16. Right center
17. Center stage
18. Left center
19. Corner
20. Front Center
21. Waki spot
22. Waki seat
23. Chorus

1. Diagram of Noh Stage

2. *SAIGYŌZAKURA* IzumiYoshio as the spirit of the cherry tree. Courtesy of the actor.

3. *IKARIKAZUKI* Sugiura Motozaburō as the ghost of Tomomori. Photograph by Ushimado Masakatsu.

4. *KAKITSUBATA* Izumi Yoshio as the spirit of the kakitsubata iris. Courtesy of the actor.

5. *GENJI KUYŌ* Takabayashi Kōji as Lady Murasaki. Photograph by Ushimado Masakatsu.

6. *ŌEYAMA* Awaya Kikuo. Courtesy of the Noh Research Archives of Musashino Women's College.

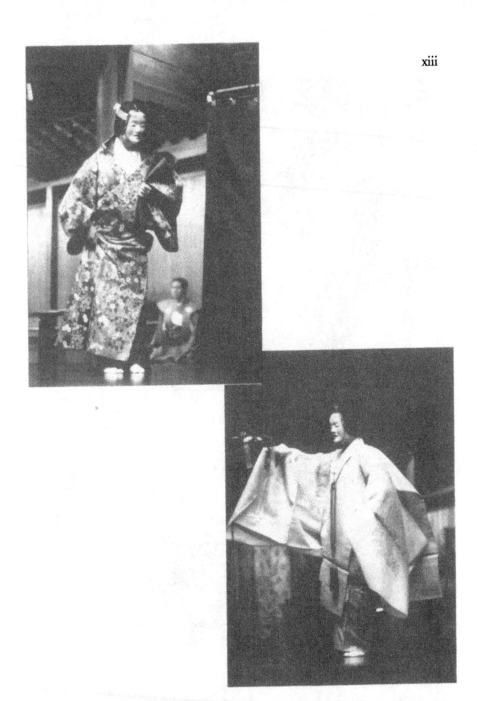

7. *MIWA* Kanze Hisao. Courtesy of the Noh Research Archives of Musashino Women's College.

8. *SEMI* Nomura Mansaku as the ghost of the Cicada. Photograph by Yoshikoshi Ken.

FOREWORD

INTRODUCTORY COMMENTS

Karen Brazell

Noh is an art form which creatively synthesizes. It braids together strands from Chinese traditions, Japanese classical court literature, mythology, legends and tales, and weaves them into a ground of arts, ideas, and events from medieval culture. The noh theater, which in the broad definition used here includes kyōgen plays, ranges from the silly to the sublime; it draws on materials from the earliest myths to contemporary domestic situations; it uses the simplest of plots (a priest meets a ghost) to produce the most complex significations (a single stage figure presents a pair of lovers, the spirit of a plant, and the concepts of enlightenment and salvation). All this is done with an economy of means (especially in terms of movement, props and music) which is quite extraordinary.

This anthology introduces the English reader to twelve plays, nine noh and three kyōgen, which reveal the variety of ways in which this theater incorporates many types of earlier texts. The plays are roughly ordered by the chronology of their source materials, an organization which, in the case of the

1

noh plays, generally parallels the order in which they are performed.[1] The first two plays, *Unoha* and *Miwa*, draw on some of Japan's earliest myths and legends. The four middle plays are based on important classical texts: the *Tales of Ise* is the major source for both *Kakitsubata* and *Unrin'in*; the *Tale of Genji* is the subject of *Genji kuyō*, and the poems of Saigyō are central to *Saigyō zakura*. *Yoshino Shizuka* and *Ikarikazuki* use material from the medieval *Tale of the Heike*, and *Ōeyama* is probably based on a late 14th century picture scroll. The three kyōgen plays, which would be performed between the noh plays, all draw on elements from the noh plays, as well as on aspects of medieval society.

The ways in which these noh and kyōgen have incorporated earlier texts, playing them off one against the other, interpreting and re-interpreting them in the course of a single play, is one of the major topics of the Afterword. That essay also discusses the plays in terms of their rhetorical strategies and the nature of their main characters. First, however, the plays are presented with as little comment as possible to allow the reader to encounter them directly. The translations have been put into similar formats with approximately the same level of information provided for each. However, no attempt has been made to standardize the style of the translations, for the richness of noh is best seen through the attempts of translators grappling to transpose it.

Producing this anthology has been a cooperative effort. The translators have worked and re-worked their contributions willingly and have provided materials and ideas about their plays. J. Philip Gabriel not only put most of the texts into the computer, editing and reformatting as he copied, but he also contributed substantial editorial comments and ideas. Monica Bethe did the drawings on each title page and the diagram of the stage, obtained the photographs, and worked on the glossary. The calligraphy on the title pages was done by the noh actor, Izumi Yoshio, and Kurosaki Akira provided expert help with the layout. Their assistance is much appreciated.

As the title of this volume suggests, it owes a debt to an earlier anthology, *Twenty Plays of the Nō Theatre*, edited by Donald Keene with the assistance of Royall Tyler. Three of the participants in this volume (Brazell, Katō and Terasaki) were students of Keene's some 20 years ago when the translations for *Twenty Plays* were being produced, and six of the present translators (Gabriel, Haynes, Horton, Jackson, Kaufman and Klein) are of the next generation, having studied noh in more recent years with Brazell. Several of them are already teaching yet another generation, a new group of scholars to whom

---

[1]Since the Tokugawa period that order has been: plays about deities (*Unoha*), warrior plays, women or wig pieces (*Kakitsubata*), miscellaneous plays (*Genji kuyō* and *Yoshino Shizuka*), and demon pieces (*Ōeyama*). The other four plays translated here may each be performed in more than one category; see the individual translations for details.

Keene's works, both his translations and his scholarship, continue to serve as an inspiration.

The contrasts between *Twenty Plays* and *Twelve Plays* reveal some of the progress the study of the noh theater has made in the last two decades in the West. In 1970 some of the most popular plays in the noh repertory had yet to be translated; by now enough translations have appeared that we can turn to less well known, yet important, plays. *Unoha*, for example, was written by Zeami, but is no longer in the active repertory and was not available in an annotated Japanese edition until 1983. Another play translated here, *Ikari-kazuki*, is still performed by two schools of actors, yet rarely appears in Japanese anthologies of noh. *Unrin'in* exists in two quite different versions, the older of which has only recently been revived. Translations of both versions are offered here. *Twelve Plays* also includes three kyōgen translations; there are none in *Twenty Plays*.

Not only have the number of English translations of plays increased dramatically since 1970, but many volumes of noh studies have also been published in English.[2] This wealth of information allows us to assume a greater understanding of noh on the part of our readers. Consequently the notes in this volume are more technical than those in *Twenty Plays*, and we include the names of the *shōdan* (segments), assuming that they will be meaningful to a growing number of readers. The expertise of the translators has also grown. As the Notes on Contributors at the end of the volume reveals, many of them have practiced noh themselves and/or have participated in the creation of "modern" noh plays. Several are preparing their own book-length studies on a variety of subjects related to the noh theater. The future of noh and kyōgen studies in English looks brighter than ever before.

[2]In addition to Keene's excellent introduction to noh (1966), see Hoff and Flindt 1973, Bethe and Brazell 1978 and 1982, Komparu 1983, and Hare 1986, as well as translations of Zeami's works by Rimer and Yamazaki 1984, Nearman 1978, 1980 and 1982-83, and Izutsu 1981. Useful volumes of translations have been done by Tyler 1978 (2 vols.) and Shimazaki (5 vols.) 1972-82.

translated by *Jeanne Paik Kaufman*

鵜

羽

UNOHA

CHARACTERS

Waki: Courtier in the service of the emperor

Wakizure: Attendant to the courtier

Shite
(act 1): A young woman who lives by the sea
(act 2): Toyotamahime, dragon princess

Tsure: A young companion to the shite in Act 1.

Kyōgen: Villager

SETTING: One autumn at the Udo cave in Hyūga province in Kyushu. The time appears to be contemporary with the writing of the play in the early 15th century.

6

AUTHOR: Zeami

CATEGORY: This would now be considered a first category or deity play.
             However Zeami labelled it a feminine style play.

PERFORMANCE PRACTICES: *Unoha* was often performed in the Muroma-
             chi period, but it was gradually withdrawn from the repertory
             during the Tokugawa period. It is not now performed by any
             school.

TEXTS: The Kōetsubon as reprinted in Itō 1983-86: 1, 171-180.

SOURCES: The tales are found in the *Kojiki* (chapters 42-45) and the
             Nihongi (ii.31-ii.50). It is unclear what later sources might have
             been used.

UNOHA (Cormorant Plumes)

Translated by Jeanne Paik Kaufman

ACT ONE

(The stage attendants carry a hut prop that is partially thatched with cormorant plumes and place it at back center stage.)

shidai music *(Waki and wakizure, both dressed in court caps, white divided skirts and lined hunting cloaks, enter and go to front center stage.)*

shidai WAKI & WAKIZURE	*(facing each other)* Whether it be the Ise or Hyūga deity, whether it be the Ise or Hyūga deity, their vows are the same.[1]
nanori WAKI	*(facing front)* I am a minister serving the present Emperor.[2] Because the Udo cave in Kyushu has been a historic spot since the age of the gods,[3] I have requested leave from my lord and am on my way there.

[1]Hyūga is the old name for Miyazaki province in Kyushu; Ise is on the Kii peninsula. The suggestion of a relationship between the two places comes from a Shinto myth in which an earth deity Sarutahiko attempts to oppose the descent of the heavenly deities. When Ame-no-Uzume, a heavenly deity, overwhelms him, he pledges to support the heavenly deities and says that their descendent should go to Hyūga and he would go to Ise (Aston 1956: 77-8, Philippi 1969: 138).

[2]*Unoha* is first mentioned in Zeami's treatise Sandō (c.1423); consequently, assuming that the dramatic present is understood to be the time of the composition of the play, the "present emperor" probably refers to Emperor Ōei (1394-1427).

[3]This natural cave which opens to the ocean on the southern coast of Kyushu, is referred to by the renga poet Bontō(an) (1349-1427) in his *Sodeshita shū*: "Udo cave is a famous place. It is in Hyūga and is the original sacred cave [where the Sun Goddess hid herself as depicted in *Miwa*]. Although it is said that this cave is in Ise, the Udo cave in Hyūga is the genuine one." (Quoted in Itō 1983: 171.)

ageuta WAKI & WAKIZURE	*(facing each other)* Our travel cloaks are made, and the paths we cover wear on, the paths we cover wear on, stretching through bay hills following what is distant with anxious hearts toward Tsukushi.[4]
tsukizerifu	At last we have arrived at Udo cave, at last we have arrived at Udo cave. *(both go to waki spot and sit)*

shin no issei music *(The shite and tsure enter. Both wear brocade robes: the shite has on a middle-aged woman's mask, the tsure, a young woman's mask. The tsure stands behind the first pine, the shite, behind the third.)*

issei SHITE & TSURE	*(facing each other)* Thatching with cormorant plumes on this day of purification, we build for the divine child a sacred hut. Take heed, you rising tides and winds. *(both face front)*
TSURE	When I ponder upon the age of the gods
SHITE & TSURE	*(facing each other)* here at Udo cave, how eternal seems this country of ours, Akitsukuni.[5]

ashirai music *(They enter the stage proper. The tsure stands at front center stage and the shite at the shite spot.)*

[4]This passage is full of puns on travel and clothes. The last phrase *kokoro o tsukushi gata* pivots on *tsukushi* which can mean "to worry, be anxious" and is also an old name for Kyushu.

[5]Akitsukuni is another name for Japan.

sashi	*(facing front)*
SHITE &	How grateful we are to recall ancient times
TSURE	when we hear of the age of the gods.
	White are the returning waves,
	crowned with purification strips;[6]
	autumn breezes rustle through the pines;
	the shrine on the shore,
	a lean-to thatched with cormorant plumes,
	is an exemplar of this long-lived country.
sageuta	Truly for a long time
	that name has been heard.
	Though we fisherwomen
	are not the heavenly maidens of long ago,
	we shall offer in abundance
	grasses from the sea
ageuta	When expressing their wishes to the gods
	when expressing their wishes to the gods
	how grateful they will be
	to learn the name of the
	Sacred Child's mother,
	Toyotamahime,
	the Princess of Ample Gems,
	of ancient times.[7]
	When gathering sea grasses
	blessed with ample dew
	even we, rustics all,
	shall so be blessed,
	shall so be blessed.

(The shite stands at center stage while the tsure goes to the corner.)

mondō	*(standing at waki spot facing the shite)*
WAKI	Hello there. I have something I'd like to ask a person from this area.

---

[6]Strips of white bark or paper called *gohei* were used in purification rituals in Shinto ceremonies.

[7]Toyo-tama-hime means literally "Ample-jewel-princess." Those who appeal to the gods are happy when they learn that her name has "ample" in it, implying that their wishes will be rewarded "amply."

SHITE   Do you mean me? What is it?

WAKI   *(looking at the hut)*
               It seems very strange that this hut
               is thatched with cormorant plumes
               on all but one side.
               (facing shite)
               Can you tell me why this is?

SHITE   Indeed, you have reason to wonder. I shall be glad to tell you
               in detail the auspicious tale of this hut thatched with cormorant
               plumes.

WAKI   Oh, how fortunate I am.
               Kindly tell me the tale.

katari   *(facing front)*
SHITE   He of the fifth generation
               of earthly deities was named
               Lord Unfinished-Cormorant-Plume-Thatch.[8]
               His divine father had descended
               to the Dragon Palace in the sea
               in search of a hook lost in a fish.
               There he betrothed Toyotamahime and
               returned to the land with the hook
               and the jewels of ebb and flow.
               Soon he began to build a temporary hut,
               for Toyotamahime was heavy with child,
               and to thatch it with cormorant plumes.
               But before he could finish the thatch,
               the child was born and hence named
               Lord Unfinished-Cormorant-Plume-Thatch.
               His birthday falls on this autumn day.[9]
               In honor of the occasion
               we are building a temporary dwelling

---

[8]The five generations of earthly deities are: 1) Amaterasu, the Sun Goddess, 2) Masakatsu Akatsu 3) Honogigini, who descended to earth with the three sacred treasures: the mirror, sword and jewel, 4) Hohodemi, who married Toyotamahime, and 5) Fuki-awaezu (thatch unfinished) who was born in that half-thatched hut by the shore, and thus so named.

[9]According to the references found in two tales of the Muromachi period, *Kamiyo monogatari* and *Tamai no monogatari*, his birth date is said to be at the end of the ninth month.

(faces the waki)
and thatching it with cormorant plumes.

kakeai	(all remain standing)
WAKI	How grateful I am to hear this tale,
	and to witness here and now
	the re-enactment of an ancient ritual:
	a purification festival,
TSURE	for the powerful deities
	whose traces extend directly
	to this very day of just rule,
WAKI	that festival once again
	rolls rapidly around to this day,
SHITE	rolling waves resound
	on this shore crying out
WAKI	the plovers flap[10]
	their wings, adding
SHITE	their feathers
WAKI	to the thatch.
ageuta	(tsure goes to back corner; waki sits)
CHORUS	Bay winds and pine breezes,
	bay winds and pine breezes,
	(shite dances to the following)
	be it a summer storm or tempest,
	the sound of the mountain wind
	matches that of the waves,
	together raising their voices.
	Thatch, thatch, quickly thatch[11]

---

[10]Plovers are usually associated with Udo. In his *Sodeshita shū* Bontō mentions a Plover Waterfall (*chidori ga taki*), a famous place near Udo. Quoted in Itō 1983: 174.

[11]The word *fuku* can mean "to blow," "to thatch" and "to grow late." Thus the original *fukeya fukeya toku fuke* can mean "Thatch, thatch, quickly thatch," or "wind is blowing, blowing, swiftly blowing," with the underlying sense that the day is ending quickly, thus they must thatch quickly as the wind rises.

the eaves and the doors
with cormorant plumes,
for the wind blows swiftly,
for the wind blows swiftly.
(goes toward front)
What concerns me are the blossoms
when the wind blows down the mountain.
How I regret the passing of time
on this night of rare chance meeting,
on this night of rare chance meeting.

[kuse]
CHORUS

(continues to dance)
How intriguing!
This indeed is one of many
strange things in this world.
Why, in Michinoku
a special cloth is woven
by threading together
the feathers of birds.[12]
In this province, they thatch
a sacred hut with cormorant plumes.
From this temporary hut
blessings sprout forth eternally
as reeds bud on the eaves;
let us cut them and thatch
this divine child's dwelling,
a visible emblem of the
eternal pledge made by the gods.[13]

rongi
CHORUS

(continues to dance)
In the settling dusk of the autumn sky,
waves break and scatter
white, pearl-like drops of dew.

---

[12]A reference to the cloth woven of feathers made in Michinoku is found in the noh play *Nishikigi*.

[13]Every word in the Japanese phrase *koya no megumi hisashi no ashikari ya yo no fushi* has at least two meanings. *Ko* means "child" while *koya* is "small hut" and the name of a place near modern Osaka which is associated with reeds; *megumi* is both "budding" and "blessing"; *hisashi* is both "long" and "eaves"; *ashikari* means "to cut the reeds," *kariya* is "temporary hut," and *ashikari ya* means "is it bad"; *yo no fushi* means "immortal world (of deities)" and refers to the reeds, literally their knots and the spaces between the knots.

> Shall we string them together
> and thatch?

SHITE
> On the eaves fall rain drops
> like leaves of words from ancient songs.
> We offer them eagerly
> to the gods
> like eagles in Unade woods.[14]
> *(looks at hut)*
> Let us gather fallen leaves
> and thatch.

CHORUS
> Let us scoop up
> the jewels of ebb and flow,
> and take advantage of this evening's
> unexpected opportunity.

SHITE
> *(looks toward the east)*
> The tide is full, the moon arisen,
> let us thatch.

CHORUS
> In the radiant moonlight
> shines the verdant *sasaki* tree
> whose brilliant color
> we shall add to our thatch.

SHITE
> Pile up on the eaves
> the forget-me-not grass.[15]

CHORUS
> Oh, we almost forgot
> to stop thatching

SHITE
> and leave a little undone,

---

[14]*Makoto matori sumu unade no mori.* This often quoted phrase comes from poem 1344 in the *Manyōshū. Matori* is an ornate way of referring to a bird: *ma* means "true or fine" and is used here to intensify *makoto* (sincere), translated here as "eagerly." *Matori* is used in reference to eagles (*washi*); however some medieval sources equate the *matori* with cormorants (Itō 1983-86: 1, 175).

[15]The *shinobugusa* (hare's foot fern) literally means "the grass of recalling" and is often associated with eaves.

CHORUS
for the name we know is
Lord Unfinished-Cormorant-Plume-Thatch,
whose hut this is.
(looks at the hut)
Leave a little undone,
leave a little undone.
As the moon's come out tonight
I, too, am revealed in its rays.
The autumn moon, lighting up the heavens,
shines upon us from the age of the gods.[16]
(sits facing waki)
Let us gaze at it till dawn breaks.

mondō
WAKI
(facing shite)
I have heard in detail why this hut was not completely thatched.
Now tell me, where are the jewels of ebb and flow?

SHITE
(facing waki)
Indeed, it seems that those jewels do exist. However, in truth,
I am not human, and I must now bid you farewell.

WAKI
If not human, then what
divine incarnation are you?
So he asks, tugging on her sleeve.

SHITE
Perhaps in the end you will know.
White waves rise in the dragon capital;
ample are the gems of a woman.
Think on this.

WAKI
The dragon capital and
a woman of abundant gems
bring to mind the name
Toyotamahime,
Princess of Ample Gems.
Are you she?

---

[16]The original sentence *Amaterasu kami yo no aki no tsuki* could also mean "the autumn moon from the age of the Sun Goddess (Amaterasu Ōmikami)."

SHITE   *(faces waki)*
Oh, I am shamefully revealed.
"'Is that a white gem?

uta
CHORUS   *(shite stands)*
Or what might it be?'
When my love asked,
I should have replied
'A dew drop' and perished."[17]
Instead, rashly
have I appeared and
am filled with shame
(uses fan to point toward audience)
for nothing separates me now
from the eyes of onlookers,
(circles stage)
not even a reed fence
(faces the waki)
blocks out the blessings of the gods. ·
So without demanding a name
just pray, pray amply,
for I am Toyotamahime,
Princess of Ample Gems.
Thus she spoke, and
(goes to shite spot and faces front)
disappeared out over the sea.
disappeared out over the sea.

(The shite exits down the bridge, followed by the tsure.)

[17]This poem is almost identical to the one in episode six of the *Tales of Ise* except for the last phrase. The poet grieves that when his lover asked him "Is it a clear gem/Or what might it be," he should have answered "a dew drop" and perished (dew connotes transience) instead of surviving to suffer her disappearance. Similarly here, Toyotamahime should have answered "a dew drop" and disappeared when she was asked by the waki for her name, but since she did not, she is now experiencing the shame of having her identity discovered.

INTERLUDE

(The kyōgen comes on stage and, in response to the inquiry of the waki, tells this tale.[18])

The Udo cave in Hyūga traces its history to the age of the gods. After seven generations of heavenly deities came the earthly deities, the fifth of whom was Lord Unfinished-Cormorant-Plume-Thatch. His father, Lord Hiko-hohodemi, made a three inch fish hook from the tip of his treasured, three-foot sword.[19] He threw in his line off this very shore, and a fish got away with the hook. Since this was a highly treasured fishhook which he wanted desperately to recover, he searched high and low for it but to no avail. Unwilling to give up, he dove into the waves and sought out the dragon palace. A woman appeared from somewhere and asked him where he was from.

"I am Lord Hiko-hohodemi, son of the fourth of the earthly deities," he answered. "Who are you?"

"You have entered the Dragon Kingdom. I am a daughter of the dragon king. I am the dragon princess called Toyotamahime," she replied.

He thought it quite marvelous. "I was fishing in the sea here, and my fish hook was taken by a fish. I have come here to recover it. Please find the hook for me, then, we shall become husband and wife," he said.

Now this princess was no ordinary being. No sooner did she set her mind to searching for the fish hook, than it was found inside the stomach of a genda fish. When he was offered the jewels of ebb and flow[20] along with the fish hook, Hiko-hohodemi was overjoyed, and since "a prince does not play with words" he kept his promise, and they became man and wife.

A short time later she became pregnant. "We must not have this child in the dragon kingdom; it should be born in the world," he said and came to this shore to build a parturition hut for her. The princess turned to her husband and said, "Promise me firmly that while I am in labor you won't look inside the hut."

[18]Versions of this story appear in the *Kojiki* (Philippi 1969: 148-158) and the *Nihongi* (Aston 1956: 92-108).

[19]Early mythology tells of two brothers; the elder had the gift of the sea, the younger the gift of the mountains. They exchanged the tools of their trade. However, the younger lost his elder brother's fish hook and attempted to replace it with one made from his treasured sword. When his brother would not accept this substitute, the younger brother entered the sea to find the lost hook. The kyōgen's tale ignores the elder brother.

[20]In the myth he uses these jewels to subdue his brother.

The hut was thatched with cormorant plumes but when one part still remained to be done, a son was born, and they named him Lord Unfinished-Cormorant-Plume-Thatch.

It has been said that cormorant plumes were used to thatch the hut in order to frighten the fish who caused the prince so much trouble by taking his fish hook.

At the time of the birth the lord's curiosity got the best of him, and he peeped inside the hut when she was in childbirth and saw her frightful appearance. She feared that he would find her disgusting thereafter and so she returned to the dragon kingdom.

Until that time, the road between this land and the dragon kingdom was like any normal road on earth. However, after her return, the way there is said to have been disrupted.

Thus it is that the Udo cave has been known as an ancient remnant of the age of the gods.

(The waki comments on the story and the kyōgen departs.)

ACT TWO

ageuta
WAKI &
WAKIZURE
(facing each other at front stage)
Rejoicing, let us now
rejoicing, let us now
rest in the shade of the pine.
The wind roars
at the hour of the tiger.[21]
We shall await the god's message,
we shall await the god's message.

deha music *(The shite appears on the bridge and goes to the shite spot on stage.)*

sashi
SHITE
(faces front)
When she was eight, the dragon princess
offered a precious gem to Buddha

---

[21]The hour of the tiger is about 4 a.m. This is the time Toyotamahime is said to have given birth. Associating the rising of the wind and the roar of a tiger is a conventional way of introducing this hour.

and achieved enlightenment.[22]
I offer the jewels of ebb and flow
that they may be treasures of the nation.

issei
SHITE   The jewel of homage, of return to Buddha
                 and original enlightenment,[23]

CHORUS   the jewel of paradise,
                 of free and perfect knowledge,[24]

SHITE   and the jewel of infinite life,
                 of harmony and miracle.

noriji
CHORUS   There are many such jewels,
                 but the truly exquisite are
                 (shite circles the stage)
                 the jewels of ebb and flow,
                 of the rise and fall
                 of land and sea.
                 Oh how grateful I am.

chūnomai *(The shite performs a dance to the accompaniment of flute and drums.
It was probably originally a version of the heavenly maiden's dance.[25])*

noriji
CHORUS   Into the sea submerge
                 the jewel of the ebb tide,
                 into the sea submerge
                 the jewel of the ebb tide,

---

[22]In chapter 12 of the *Lotus Sutra*, the daughter of the dragon king, barely eight years of age, was presented with the challenge that since a woman's body is impure, no woman could become a Buddha. She offered a precious gem to Buddha, was instantly turned into a man and thus achieved enlightenment (Hurvitz 1976: 199-121).

[23]*Namu* (revere, hail, pay homage to) is a transliteration of the Sanskrit *namas*, which is often translated as *kimyō* (take refuge in, return to). This begins a catalogue of jewels.

[24]This refers to one of the 48 vows Amida made in the process of establishing his Western Paradise.

[25]Zeami depicts this dance in his *Nikkyoku santai zu* (Illustrations of the two arts and three styles). The drawing is reproduced in Rimer and Yamazaki (1984: liv). For a discussion of this dance see Itō 1983-86: 1, 411-412.

and behold! dry beach
where once was sea.
The waves rolling in are
(indicates the waves with fan)
blown back by a gale.
(beckons with the fan)
The dry beach extends
a thousand leagues
(holds up the fan to look into distance)
spread with pure white sand
sparkling like snow
far into the distance.

hanomai *(A brief dance to instrumental music.)*

noriji *(offering the open fan)*
SHITE Then place the jewel of the flow tide
(goes to the stage front and kneels)
into the sea,

CHORUS then place the jewel of the flow tide
into the sea.
(rises)
Now the wind rises
in the offing,
fiercely blowing on and
(beckons with the fan)
causing tidal waves
to flood the land,
to rise and to overflow.
How easy to turn
(looks down at front)
mountains into seas,
(looks up to left)
seas into mountains.
The jewels of ebb and flow
(raises fan and circles the stage)
are wondrous treasures
and yet, my heart desires
the true jewel of enlightenment,
pure as the heart of a holy man.
(turns toward waki)
Please grant me this wish!

Please grant me this wish!
(waves fan and goes to shite spot)
With her entreaty deep as the ocean
she immediately
(concluding stamps)
enters into the waves.

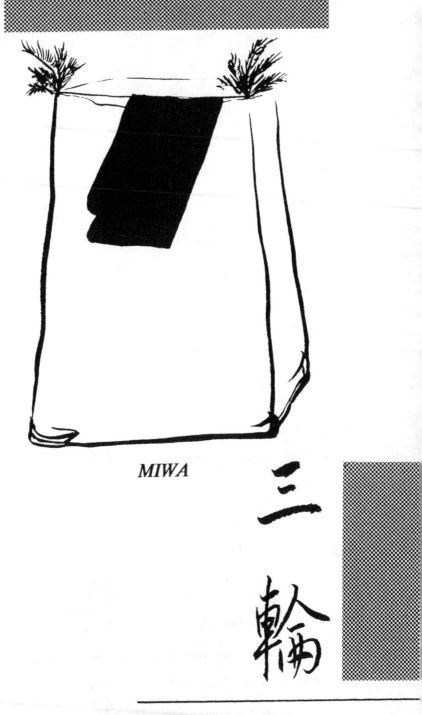

MIWA

三
輪

translated by **Monica Bethe**

CHARACTERS

Waki: High Priest Genpin

Shite
(act 1):   Woman of Miwa
(act 2):   Goddess of Miwa

Kyōgen: Local man

SETTING: An autumn day in the 9th century at the foot of Mt. Miwa in Nara Prefecture. In act one the prop represents the hut of a priest, in act two the shrine of the god of Miwa and the cave into which the Sun Goddess disappears.

AUTHOR: Unknown, traditionally attributed to Zeami.

CATEGORY: Now included in the fourth category as a sacred dance piece. The sacred dance, kagura, is generally performed by a deity or a priestess possessed by a deity. *Miwa* is also performed as a first or third category play.

24

PERFORMANCE PRACTICES: Currently performed by all schools. The numerous variant performances involve alterations in costuming, placement of the kagura dance, music (mainly in the kagura), choreography and staging.

TEXT: The translation is based primarily on Yokomichi and Omote, 1960-63: 2, 329-33, but draws also from Koyama et al. 1973, Sanari 1930-31, and Kanze 1980. Stage directions are a composite based on recent performances by the Kanze, Kongō, and Kita schools as well as notes in Yokomichi and Omote. Costume notes come primarily from Kanze.

SOURCES: Legends about the marriage of the Miwa goddess appear in the *Kojiki* chapter 66 and the *Nihongi* V.13 (in this story husband is a snake). Stories about Genpin appear in the setsuwa collections, *Gōdanshō*, *Hosshinshū*, and *Kojidan*. The Amaterasu story is in both the *Kojiki* (chapter 17) and the *Nihongi* (I.38-I.41).

TRANSLATIONS: French, Steinilber-Oberlin, 1929; Péri 1944: 291-313; German, Gundert 1925.

MIWA (Three Circles)

Translated by Monica Bethe

ACT ONE

(After the musicians enter two attendants bring on the stage prop, a square bamboo frame covered by a cloth with small branches of cedar attached to the top front corners, and place it at back center stage.)

nanori *flute music (The waki dressed in a black cap, a plain, small-sleeved, satin kimono and a travelling cloak walks down the bridge to the shite spot.)*

nanori WAKI	*(facing front)* I am the high priest Genpin,[1] living in the shadow of Mt. Miwa. Recently a woman has been coming here from I know not where, bearing a holy branch and holy water.[2] If she comes today, I think I shall inquire about her and ask her name. *(goes and sits at waki spot)*

shidai music *(The shite appears on the bridge wearing a middle-aged woman's mask, a tightly draped brocade kimono and carrying a branch, or in some performances a water bucket, in her left hand and a rosary in the right. She walks to the shite spot and turns to face the prop.)*

---

[1] Genpin sōzu (739-818). Both the *Hosshinshū* (chapter 1) and the *Kojidan* describe Genpin as "a man of incomparable intelligence" and mention that he moved from the Yamashina Temple to a small grass hut at Miwa River, the name of the Hase River where it passes north of Mt. Miwa. Today Genpin's hut may be visited just to the south of Hibara Shrine and somewhat to the north of Miwa Shrine.

[2] The "holy branch" of Buddhism is the *shikimi*, a fragrant evergreen, which is used to make incense. Because name of the sacred tree of Shintō (*sakaki*) is written with a Japanese character combining the tree radical and the character for deity, *shikimi* may be written with a character combining "tree" and "Buddha." It is common to offer a sacred branch and water (*aka no mizu*, which simply means water given as an offering) at a temple or shrine. Usually only one is represented visually on the noh stage.

26

shidai
SHITE   No path at the foot of Mt. Miwa
no path at the foot of Mt. Miwa
so I visit the depths of Hibara field.[3]

nanorizashi   *(faces front)*
Truly, age is unfair.
As I linger uselessly in this world,
how many springs and falls have blossomed
without meaning or purpose?
Empty months turn to years,
moons wax and wane, while this woman
lives on in the village of Miwa.
Still, in the shadows of this mountain
lives the high priest Genpin, a noble man,
to whom I always bring holy water and a
sacred branch. Today, too, I set forth.

kakeai
WAKI   In the evening a solitary moon
crowns the mountain peak,
in the morning a single cloud
drifts from the cave mouth.[4]
Sad indeed is the figure guarding the hill,
for no one visits in deepening autumn.[5]

mondō   *(standing at the shite spot)*
SHITE   Hello, I've come to call on the occupant of this hut.

WAKI   Are you the one who comes here regularly?

SHITE   The shadow of the mountain
slips through the gate:
no pushing will shove it aside.

[3]Hibara is to the north of Mt. Miwa. Path refers both to the physical road and to the path of the Buddha.

[4]A Japanese version of lines from a Chinese poem in the *Hyakuren shōkai*.

[5]A slight variation of a poem by High Priest Genpin anthologized in the *Shokukokinshū*, the 11th imperial waka anthology compiled in 1265. The word *sōzu* (translated here as "figure") means both priest and scarecrow.

WAKI	The light of the moon spreads over the gravel: no sweeping will brush it away.[6]
SHITE & WAKI	The constant chirping of the birds, companions to our old age in the stillness of a mountain dwelling.

sageuta *(The shite approaches the waki, kneels, lays down her branch and prays with rosary.)[7]*

CHORUS   Pushing open the brushwood door
I bear a cut branch as offering.
Please save me from my sins.

ageuta   Autumn cold penetrates the window
autumn cold penetrates the window.
Wind through the pines, rain at the eaves,
leaves blanketing the garden;
will weeds block off the gate?
The sound of water trickling under moss
--silence.
This mountain dwelling, so lonely.

mondō
SHITE   Your reverend, I have a request to make. The autumn nights are chilly. Would you give me one of your robes?

WAKI   Certainly. I'll give you this one.

(He lays a robe, which has been brought to him by the stage attendant, down on the stage for the shite, who picks it up and drapes it over her left arm.)

SHITE   Thank you very much. And now, I must take my leave.

(The shite stands and starts to leave, then halts at the shite spot in response to the waki's question.)

---

[6]These two couplets are a quote from a Chinese poem in the *Hyakuren shōkai*.

[7]The first chorus lines are often accompanied by a short dance. Only some performances of *Miwa* include this abstract dance.

WAKI   Wait a minute. You're a stranger, please tell me where you
              live.
              *(Shite turns to face waki, takes a step towards him with arms
              out.)*

SHITE   My house is in the village of Miwa, close to the foot of the
              mountain--just as the verse says, "my cottage snuggles
              against the foot of the mountain, if you long to see me, do
              come,"[8] and should you have doubts of the whereabouts, ask
              for

CHORUS   this sign, "cedars standing at the gate".
              Please do come and visit,
              she says, and, as if extinguished, vanishes.

*(The shite circles right and disappears into the prop. A stage attendant drapes the
robe over the front of the prop while the kyōgen, a villager dressed in a matching
vest and long trailing trousers comes to the shite spot.)*

INTERLUDE

KYŌGEN   I live in the village of Miwa in the province of Wa. In hopes of
              having a long cherished desire fulfilled, I decided to worship
              at Miwa Shrine for seven days. Today is the seventh and
              therefore truly sacred, so I must hurry along my way.
              (walks around the stage)
              It may be improper for someone of my low birth to talk
              about the gods, but the lineage of the god here is exalted.
              When the primal father and mother gods, Izanagi and Izan-
              ami lay in the heavenly moss gardens of Iwakura and spoke
              of love, they bore one daughter and three sons. The daugh-
              ter was the Sun Goddess, and the three sons were the Moon
              God, Hiruko, and Susanō. The child of Susanō, known both
              as Great Snake and the Lord of Great Things, is the god of

---

[8]This is poem 982 of the *Kokinshū*. The last line appears in the chorus section below. The
Kokinshū poem has no topic and is anonymous. However, there is a variation of the poem in
Toshiyori zuinō which links it directly with the deity of Miwa: "This is a poem sent by the deity of
Miwa to the deity of Sumiyoshi" (quoted in Yokomichi and Omote 1960-63: 2, 440).

this shrine.[9] Although he responds generously to offerings, he has neither a home nor any other embodiment except the holy cedars.[10]

(arrives at the corner)

While I have been talking to myself, I have reached the shrine.

(faces the prop and kneels to pray)

Thanks be to heaven. My wishes are fulfilled through my seven days of worship. I leave satisfied.

(gets up to leave, approaches the prop, sees the garment hanging on it and stops) This is strange! A robe is hanging from one of the branches of the sacred tree. I could swear it belongs to the priest Genpin who lives at the foot of the mountain. I wonder why it has been hung here. Indeed, it's so strange, I think I shall visit Genpin and ask him about it.

(goes to center stage; kneels facing waki)

Please excuse me for not having visited you recently.

WAKI   What has kept you away?

KYŌGEN   Although I wanted to come every day, I was occupied with seven days of pilgrimages to Miwa Shrine to have a wish fulfilled. Today was the last day, and all has gone well. However, it is not that which has brought me here directly from the shrine. Rather, there is a robe hanging on one of the branches of the sacred tree, a robe which looks suspiciously like your Reverend's. I thought it peculiar, and so came to ask why it might be hanging there.

WAKI   What? You say that you saw the cloak of a humble priest like myself hanging on the branch of the sacred tree?

KYŌGEN   That's right.

---

[9]The Sun Goddess (literally "Lighter of the heavens," read Amaterasu or Tenshō) is the original ancestor of all Japanese emperors and is housed in Ise Shrine. Her youngest brother, Susanō, ruler over the earth, angered her, leading to her disappearance into a cave (related later in the play). The God of Miwa (Ōanamuji or Ōmononushi) is the nephew of the Sun Goddess. For a detailed discussion of the mythology behind the play see Péri 1944: 291-97.

[10]Although invisible, Shinto Gods may inhabit rocks, trees, and other natural objects. These then become their "god body" or *shintai*. The double cedars are thus both a natural shrine and a *shintai*.

WAKI   I think I know the reason. Lately a woman has been coming here from somewhere bringing holy water and a branch. Today when she came, I asked her where she lived, but scarcely had she said, "Please visit me using a gate of cedars as a guide," than she vanished.

KYŌGEN   This is the most miraculous thing I have heard in a long time. Still, there is no reason to doubt it. In this degenerating world, it does not seem strange that a god should visit a high priest in order to save mankind. That must be why the deity temporarily took on the guise of a woman and brought you holy water each day. It is said that even the highest gods suffer from the five degenerations and three torments.[11] It could be that the deity requested your robe in order to escape from some suffering or other. If you have any doubts, come to the shrine with me and see for yourself that your robe is hanging on the holy tree.

WAKI   I haven't encountered anything so intriguing for quite some time. I think I shall walk over and have a look at the robe.

KYŌGEN   Then I shall follow along.

WAKI   Anyone else? Please come along if you wish.

KYŌGEN   Coming.
              (retreats to his spot on the bridge)

ACT TWO

ageuta   *(stands and walks toward the prop)*
WAKI   Setting out from my hut
              setting out from my hut
              soon I spy Miwa village.
              Perhaps in the shadow of the mountain here
              she waits, yet "the pine is not the marker,

[11]According to Buddhist ideas, deities are not enlightened, but rather reside in a heavenly realm (*ten*) where they enjoy a pleasant life, but are still subject to death and rebirth. The five signs of degeneration (*gosui*: dirty clothes, withering flowers, foul smells, etc.) appear before a heavenly being dies. The three torments or three kinds of heat (*sannetsu*) are sufferings undergone by dragons, who like deities are seen as superior beings.

rather a thicket of cedar,"[12]
and a sacred gate, where can they be?
and a sacred gate, where can they be?

(He sees the robe, takes a step forward and sees the poem, which is not represented concretely on stage.)

WAKI   This is strange. On the double trunk of this cedar I see the robe which I gave that woman. However, on closer inspection I see gold letters decorating the hem. They form a poem:

genoei   *(reads the poem, then returns to waki spot)*
Three circles
clean and clear:
the Chinese cloak,
not to be thought of as given,
nor as taken.[13]

jōnoei   *(singing inside the covered prop)*
SHITE   Since even sacred
deities have desires
I, like a human, rejoice
at this chance meeting.

---

[12]In the 51st story of the 24th volume of *Konjaku monogatari* Akasome Emon sends a poem with these lines in it to her husband. That poem is then quoted in the *Toshiyori zuinō* passage which is the source for the story told below in the *kuse* (see note 8 above). Sometime in the mid Edo period, however, the noh text was changed from *matsu wa shirushi mo nakarikeri* (pine is not the marker) to *matsu wa tokiwa no iro zo kashi* (the pine with its ever lasting color!). This was presumably done to show respect to the Matsudaira (*matsu* is pine) branch of the Tokugawa family. In recent times, all but the Hōshō school have reverted to the original wording (Yokomichi & Omote 1963: 440).

[13]The following poem is a variation on one which appears in the first section of the *Gōdanshō* where it was composed by Genpin when a woman gave him a robe. The opening phrase, *mitsu no wa wa* (three circles), has embedded in it the name Miwa and refers to the three aspects of the transaction: the gift, giver and receiver. It also alludes to the Buddhist concept of *sanrin* (written with the same characters as *miwa*) or the three agents of human action: the body, the mouth and the spirit. The second line, *kiyoku kiyoki zo* (clean and clear), suggests the purity of the deed that erases self, attachment and expectation. *Karakoromo* (Chinese cloak) in the third line has embedded in it the meaning "empty" (*kara*, which can also be read *kū*) and refers to "empty (unattached) alms", those in which neither giver nor receiver have a vested interest (Sanari 1930-31: 2983). Mark Nearman discusses Zenchiku's allusion to this poem (1986: 45-46).

kakeai   *(standing at waki spot and facing prop)*
WAKI   How very strange, from the shadows of this cedar wafts a wondrous voice. I pray you, fulfill the wishes of mankind and reveal yourself. Tears of deepest gratitude dampen my ink-black robe.

SHITE   Although ashamed of my looks
I shall appear before you, priest.
Please save me from my sins.

WAKI   No, no. Guilt and sins abide in humans.
You are a wondrous deity,

SHITE   a means of salvation for mankind.

WAKI   For a while I wander bewildered,

SHITE   with human heart

(During the following song, the cloth is removed from the hut, revealing the seated shite dressed in a lacquer hat, white satin kimono, red, or in some cases white, broad divided skirts, and a gauze cloak, also sometimes white. The mask is one for a goddess, either masugami or zōonna.)

ageuta   *(waki kneels to pray)*
CHORUS   Seen in the form of a woman,
the deity of Miwa
seen in the form of a woman,
the deity of Miwa
dressed not in the garb of a priestess[14]
but attired as a priest
with lacquer hat and hunting cloak
draped over skirts.
Most gratifying
this fresh vision of the sacred.

[14]A priestess, or miko, would wear a *chihaya* (sleeveless festive cloak), waist length in front with a longer piece trailing down in back. Today this is generally white with stenciled patterns of grasses and flowers. The miko wears this with red divided skirts. The standard noh costume today approximates this, and consequently goes against the text. In variant performances, the text is sometimes taken literally and the shite is attired as a male.

kuri	*(shite stands and goes out of prop[15])* Ancient myths of the gods teach mankind throughout the ages; stories of various kinds are a means to salvation for the world.
sashi SHITE	Especially in this island country where people are filled with reverence and awe[16] the power of the deities is great.
CHORUS	They mingle with the impure dust of life briefly defiling their souls: for example, years ago in the land of Yamato lived a husband and wife whose love, like the green camellia remained unchanged for year after year.[17]
kuse	*(shite dances, first going to the corner, then circling left to center stage)* It happened that the husband came each evening, but was never seen by day. In an intimate exchange one night his wife asked, "Why for all these years have you come only in the blackness of night? What is wrong with the day? This seems extremely strange. Have we not sworn a mutual vow of eternal love?" Her husband replied,

[15]In several variant performances the shite remains seated for part, or almost all of the *kuse* scene (*kuri/sashi/kuse*). Making the *kuse* seated rather than danced shifts the visual emphasis of the play onto the following section where the story of Amaterasu is acted out. It also emphasizes that these are merely stories being told to amuse or enlighten the priest Genpin.

[16]This line appears also in *Yoshino Shizuka* kuri and in *Makiginu*.

[17]The unchanging color of the love between husband and wife is introduced by the phrase *yachiyo o komeshi tamatsubaki* (the jeweled camellia that lasts eight thousand ages), which is a rephrasing of a line from a poem by Jien (1155-1225) recorded in his personal collection the *Shūgyokushū*, where it is used to describe the long and prosperous reign of the emperor.

"In truth, I am ashamed of my appearance.
In fear that the world will learn of it,
I shall cease to visit you.
Our love ends this very night."
Gently though he spoke,
the separation loomed sadly.
Wanting to know where he went,
she threaded a needle with a spool of bast
(mimes threading needle by lifting fan)
and stuck it in his hem
that she might follow the thread to him.

SHITE

(opens the fan, zigzags to stage front)
Long are young willow branches,[18]

CHORUS

strings of jewels, spiders' webs,
and frail is the thread unwinding,
round and round it goes till
(mimes unreeling the thread and following it to in front of the prop)
at the mountain base, at the sacred gate,
it stops among low cedar branches.
How amazing!
Was the man I loved this tree?
(goes forward; lowers fan to front)
Three loops of thread remained
and from these derives the name
The Cedar of Three Circles.[19]
(circles left to downstage center)

---

[18]This line and the two that follow are a stream of associated words and puns which defy any grammatical analysis. The willow (*aoyagi*) and the spider (*sasagani*) are both related to thread; the spinning of a web by a spider was thought to indicate the arrival of a lover (i.e. *Kokinshū* poem 1110, originally in the *Nihongi*, Aston 1896: 320). The phrase *musubu ya hayatama no ono* (translated simply "strings of jewels") contains the names of a pair of gods at Kumano: Musubu Miya is an alternate name for the Nachi deity Fusemi and Hayatama no Ono Mikoto is the name of the deity at Shingū. In addition, the character used for *ono* means snake. It thus suggests that the husband's true form was that of a snake, and indeed one of the names of the deity of Miwa is Great Snake (see the Interlude). In the *Kojiki* version of the tale the snake identity is disclosed by the thread passing through the keyhole to leave the room (Philippi 1969: 204).

[19]*Miwa no shirushi no sugi*, literally "the cedar is the sign of Miwa (Three Circles)." That is to say the cedar is the god body (*shintai*) of the deity worshipped at Miwa shrine. *Sugi* (cedar) is embedded in *sugishi yo* (the past). Visually also the three loops of thread suggest a coiled snake.

                    I am embarrassed to tell this tale
                    of things that happened long ago.

rongi   Truly gratifying.
                    This tale strengthens one's trust
                    in the way of Buddha's law.

SHITE   *(standing in front of the prop)*
                    Well then, another tale
                    from the world of deities
                    will be revealed in all its fullness
                    to solace the high priest.

(The stick drum begins to play and continues until the final song.)

SHITE   The story of the rock cave began with
                    the need to lure out the hiding deity.[20]
                    The eight myriad dances by the gods
                    were the genesis of *kagura*.[21]

(The shite goes to the shite spot closing the fan, receives a purification wand from the stage attendant, then bows and purifies the place with the wand.)

ei   Flourishing sacred sleeves[22]

kagura dance   *(At the shite spot he performs several introductory stamps to the calls of the drummers. These originated in purification rites. The shite then dances around the stage to instrumental music. The first three sections of the dance, which are stately and rhythmical, are performed to special kagura music.*

[20]According to the myth, the world darkened when the angered Sun Goddess disappeared into a cave. The story appears in slightly different versions in both the *Kojiki* (chapter 17) and the *Nihongi* (1.38-1.41). To lure her out, one of the young female deities, Ameno Uzume no Mikoto, stripped and danced wildly, stamping on an overturned bucket. The laughter of the deities tempted the Sun Goddess to peep out of the cave. The story is given as the prototype for the performing arts in Japan.

[21]*Kagura* or "sacred music" is the generic name for Shinto dance and music.

[22]*Chihayaburu* is a pillow word for deities. *Chihaya* is also the garment that a priestess wears when performing rituals, and *furu* also means to wave.

For the last two sections, done to fast god music, the shite exchanges the purifica-tion wand for a fan.[23])

[kuri]	*(goes to corner using fan to mime shoving door closed)*
SHITE	The heavenly rock door is pulled shut:
CHORUS	the goddess has entered leaving no trace,
	the world turns instantly,
	impenetrably dark.
	(covers face with fan and sleeve, circles right and faces prop)
SHITE	The eight myriad deities
	grieve before the cave.
	Then their dances and music[24]
noriji	*(The shite kneels at center stage, mimes opening the door, then stands and dances standard abstract movements, circling the stage to the left.)*
CHORUS	tempt the Sun Goddess to open
	the rock door a crack
	and the impenetrable dark cloud
	brightens with the light of sun and moon,
	making all the faces appear white.[25]
SHITE	How amusing the gods' songs!
CHORUS	How wondrous
	the story of their beginning!
uta	The deities of Ise and Miwa
	the deities of Ise and Miwa

[23]In the lower lineage schools this entire dance is performed to kagura music, and the shite holds the wand the whole time. In some variant performances the kagura dance comes later in the text, and a short *iroe* dance is done here.

[24]In variant performances the *kagura* may come here. Then it becomes the dance for the Sun Goddess and is followed directly by her opening the cave door. In that case, towards the end of the *kagura* dance, the shite goes down the bridge and then rushes back from the third pine, enters the prop (now representing the cave) as the chorus begins to sing, and opens its door to peep out, in effect changing roles from the entertainer to the Sun Goddess.

[25]"Faces appear white" (*omote shirojiro*) in this line links to "amusing" (*omoshiro*) in the next, since the same characters are used to write both.

are but one being in two forms.[26]
What is left to tell?
As the dark cave door broke open,
(spreads arms looking up toward curtain[27])
so night now breaks into dawn.
(circles right to shite spot, stamps[28])
From sacred revelation
awakening, to take unwilling leave,
awakening, to take unwilling leave.

[26]The source of the idea that the Miwa and Ise deities were originally one is unknown. Péri mentions that Hibara Shrine north of Genpin's hut is dedicated to Amaterasu (1944: 298), and one version of the Interlude states that the god of Miwa is "of one body" with Amaterasu.

[27]The cloud pattern used here is often used for looking into the distance at the sunrise or sunset. It was also used to mime the opening of the cave door earlier.

[28]For the last three lines the shite may exit down the bridge, performing the concluding stamps in front of the curtain.

UNRIN'IN

雲林院

translated by Earl Jackson, Jr.

CHARACTERS

Waki:	Kinmitsu, an inhabitant of Ashiya
Wakizure:	His attendants
Shite	
(act 1):	An old man
(act 2):	Ariwara no Narihira in newer version
	Fujiwara no Mototsune in older version
Tsure	
(act 2):	Empress Kōshi, older version only
Kyōgen:	A villager
SETTING:	Unrin Temple in Kyoto on a spring day.
AUTHOR:	Unknown, but the play dates from Zeami's time.
CATEGORY:	This is considered a fourth-category, entertainment play or a pseudo third-category, woman play.

PERFORMANCE PRACTICES: The newer version is currently performed by all schools except Konparu. The older version has just recently been revived.

TEXT: This play exists in two versions. The newer one is translated in its entirety from the text in Koyama et al. 1973-75: 1, 441-50. Sanari 1930-31: 457-470 was also consulted. The first acts of the two versions are very similar; the few significant differences are given in the footnotes. However, the very different, older second act is fully translated from Yokomichi and Omote 1960-63: 1, 154-156.

SOURCES: The *Tales of Ise* (especially episodes 6, 9 and 12) and medieval commentaries on that work (most notably the *Waka chikenshū*).

UNRIN'IN (The Unrin Temple)

Translated by Earl Jackson, Jr.

ACT ONE

(The stage attendants place a cherry tree prop at center stage front. In the older version a tomb prop is also brought in and put at back center stage.)

shidai music *(The waki and wakizure enter. The waki wears white divided skirts and a sedge hat. He has a bag containing a scroll of the Tales of Ise hung around his neck. The wakizure wear matching vest and long trousers.)*

shidai	*(facing each other at stage front)*
WAKI &	The wisteria on the pine blooms
WAKIZURE	purple the wisteria blooms the pine
	purple the cloud-covered forest
	I will visit.[1]
nanori	*(holds hat, faces front)*
WAKI	I am Kinmitsu, from the village of Ashiya, in the province of Tsu.[2] One night, while pouring over the *Tales of Ise* which I have loved since childhood, I received a strange, ghost-filled dream. Therefore I have decided to visit the capital.[3]

---

[1]*Fuji saku matsu mo murasaki no/fuji saku matsu mo murasaki no/kumo no hayashi o tazunen.* The word *murasaki*, "purple," simultaneously belongs to the line preceding it and following it in both its occurrences. "The pine blooms purple," and "purple, the wisteria," as well as: "the wisteria blooms the pine purple," and "purple, the cloud-covered forest." The phrase *murasaki no* ("of purple") also suggests Murasakino, the Murasaki field, where the Unrin Temple was located. *Kumo no hayashi* is the native Japanese reading for the Chinese characters in the temple's name.

[2]Near Ashiya City, between modern Osaka and Kobe.

[3]The *nanori* of the older version of the play is quite different: "I am Kinmitsu, from the village of Ashiya, in the province of Tsu. Long ago in my youth I fondly read the *Tales of Ise* and received secret instruction on this work from a certain personage. One night in a dream I saw a man in formal attire and a lady in a scarlet robe beneath the blossoms perusing a volume of the *Tales of Ise*. When I asked an old man standing in the shadows of the trees about the pair, he informed me that the man was the hero of the tales, the Middle Captain Narihira, that the woman was the Empress of the Second Ward, and that the place was the cloudy forest of the Murasaki Plain in the Capital. At that, I awoke from the dream. Because it was such a portentous dream, I have decided to hasten to the capital and visit this place."

42

sashi
WAKI   While blossoms open anew in the sun
drinking in the blessings
of the first light,
while weary birds
return to their nests
through lightly clouded spring evenings[4]
I hasten to the moon radiant capital.

sageuta
WAKI &   *(puts on hat again and faces wakizure)*
WAKIZURE   Travelling eastward from Ashiya village
The moon that's left[5]
Above the Western sea.
How far is the tideswept beach of Hiruko![6]
How far is the tideswept beach of Hiruko!

ageuta   Through the pine shadows
Amagasaki decked in smoke,[7]
Amagasaki decked in smoke
fisherfires lighting up the dusk--where?
"In Naniwa harbor they bloom
the blossoms of the trees
from their winter slumber."[8]
It is truly Naniwa I see
The road to the capital so distant
The cherries cloud
the forest at which we have arrived.
We have arrived

---

[4]Based on a Japanese translation of a Chinese poem by Sugawara Fumitoki (899-981), number 83 in the *Wakan rōeishū*.

[5]See note 37.

[6]*Shio no hiruko* (Hiruko of the tides)" also contains the meaning *shio no hi* (tide ebbs) which is associated with the sea of the previous line and the images of fishermen and salt fires that follow.

[7]*Kemuri o kazuku Amagasaki* (smoke covers Amagasaki). *Kazuku* also means "dives," forming a link with *ama* meaning "fisherman" or "diver." Amagasaki is to the east of present-day Nishinomiya.

[8]The first three lines from an anonymous poem from the Japanese preface to the *Kokinshū*. Naniwa is the old name for Osaka.

at the cloud covered forest.
(takes steps to indicate journey)

tsukizerifu
WAKI

(holding hat he faces front)
Because we have hurried, we have already reached the Unrin Temple of the capital. The blossoms here are so abundant I think I shall step among them and break off a branch.

WAKIZURE A fine idea.

[ ]
WAKI

(puts on his hat, advances to center stage)
As the poem says,
"Far off I see a dwelling
Since there are blossoms
I shall enter."[9]
So shall I step into the shade of this tree and break off a branch...
(starts toward waki spot)

(The shite enters wearing an old man's mask and wig and a plaid gown under a travel cloak.)

[unnamed]
SHITE

(slowly comes unto the bridge)
Who would break off a branch?
Just as the day dispelled the morning mist
so clear is the evening sky
of this spring night.
Especially tranquil can be seen Mt. Arashi
From which, despite its name,
comes no wind.[10]
(stops at third pine)
Yet--what scatters the blossoms?
Do they fall from the breeze
of a nightingale's wing?[11]
The murmurings of the pines?
Is it a person who disturbs them?

[9]Based on a Chinese poem by Po Chü-i, *Wakan rōeishū*, number 115.

[10]*Arashi* means "storm."

[11]The image of petals scattered by a nightingale's wing is recurrent in Japanese literature, an example is *Kokinshū* poem 109 by the priest Sosei. References to his poems are important in this play, as he was in residence at Unrin Temple.

(resumes walking)
Is it none of these?
Perhaps a breeze beneath the trees?
Oh--how it touches the heart
the sight of scattered blossoms.
(stops at first pine)

mondō   *(moves to shite spot)*
SHITE   Ah hah! As I suspected--a person! Thief![12]
      Stand back!
      (steps forward)

WAKI   Whether I ask for them or simply take them--either is a sign
      of my appreciation of their beauty. How zealously you guard
      blossoms sure to fall!

SHITE   They are certain to fall
      the storm is sure to bring about their end
      yet even this only scatters the petals
      you would carry away an entire branch
      more harm than awaits them from the wind.
      (stands at shite spot and faces waki)

WAKI   But the priest Sosei writes:
      "Cherry flowers, should I merely look
      and tell others of the beauty?
      I will break off a branch
      as a gift for those at home."[13]

SHITE   There is such a poem,
      but there is also the poem,
      "Spring wind--pray, avert your path
      from the cherries
      I would see
      whether they will their own demise."[14]
      The poet has also written,
      "I would not trade

---

[12]*rakkarōzeki:* "flower thief," a rather stiff Chinese compound from *Wakan rōeishū* number 129 by Tomotsuna. Also appears in the noh play *Kagetsu.*

[13]*Kokinshū* poem 55.

[14]*Kokinshū* 85 by Fujiwara Yoshikaze (flourished around 900).

one moment of a spring evening,
the blossoms fragrant and luminous
in the radiance of the moon
for one thousand pieces of gold."[15]
I hold these blossoms as a treasure more
precious than stores of jewels beyond
reckoning,[16] and will not permit you to break them off.

kakeai
WAKI   Indeed what you say is true. Because "flowers have a mute
charm,"[17] a desire for them enfolds the viewer

SHITE   "the reflections of the flowers
quiver on the ripples of a wave
moving their lips
though they themselves say nothing"

WAKI   flowers are precious

SHITE   *(takes one step toward waki)*
we must affirm always.

ageuta
CHORUS   preserving the branches
for the springs to come
(moves to stage right)
breaking off a branch
for those who have not seen the blossoms
(faces waki)
both the treasuring and the longing
betray a heart moved by beauty
conflicting desires clash
as do the colors[18]

[15]Based on the poem *Ch'ün ye*, "Spring Evening," by Su Tung P'o (1037-1101).

[16]Based on *Wakan rōeishū* poem 116 by Sugawara Fumitoki.

[17]Based on *Wakan rōeishū* 117 by Sugawara Fumitoki. This poem, which is continued in
the next shite line, also appears in the plays *Saigyōzakura* and *Hōshigahaha* translated in this
volume.

[18]The word in the original is *iro*, which basically means "color," but has additional meanings ranging from "form" in Buddhist metaphysics to "sexual passion." Here I translate it as
both "color" and "desire" to capture the use of two of its meanings, and to take advantage of the
double meaning of the English verb "clash."

the willow and cherry interweave
spring brocade in the capital
(circles left to the shite spot)
spring brocade in the capital[19]

mondō
SHITE

Traveller, from where have you come?

WAKI

I am Kinmitsu, from the village of Ashiya in the province of Tsu. Since my childhood I have fondly read the *Tales of Ise*. One night, in a dream, in the shade of certain blossoms, I saw a lady wearing crimson trousers and a man in ceremonial dress holding a volume of the *Tales of Ise*. When I asked an old man nearby who these people were, he answered that the man was the hero of the *Tales of Ise* the Captain Narihira, and the woman was the Empress of the Second Ward.[20] The setting was in the shadows at the foot of Mt. Kita in the capital, at the cloud covered forest of Musashi Plain. At this, I awoke. Because it was such a wondrous occurrence, I have ventured all this way.

SHITE

(faces the waki)
Ah, this can only mean Narihira has understood your heart and will impart the secrets of the *Tales of Ise* to you. This evening rest here and await the dream which left you too soon. *(faces front)*

kakeai
WAKI

Oh, How happy I am! Spreading my robes upon the ground, I will rest here.

SHITE

The blossoms ever piling into flowery robes, if you await another dream, why should a revelation fail to appear?

WAKI

You have explained so much, who are you?

[19]Based on *Kokinshū* poem 56 by Sosei.

[20]Ariwara no Narihira (825-80), one of the six poetic geniuses. The Empress, Fujiwara Koshi was the niece of the Empress of the Fifth Ward, Fujiwara Junshi, and the consort of the Emperor Seiwa. According to the legend, she had an affair with Narihira before Seiwa reached puberty. This couple also appears in the play *Kakitsubata* translated in this volume.

SHITE From my age and appearance, why do you not recognize "the man of old?"[21] *(faces waki)*

WAKI Then, are you Narihira?

SHITE Hmmm.....

ageuta *(faces front)*
CHORUS If I could name myself
and even
if I could name myself
in the evening glow
(waki goes to waki seat)
moved by the blossoms
I appear half hidden
like the moon among the branches.[22]
faces waki)
If you truly love the past
(goes to stage right)
spread your single cloak
and sleep beneath the shadows
of the blossom decked branches.
When I show you my true form
(faces waki)
then your confusion should clear away
(faces front)
he said, and vanished
into the fine mist of an evening sky.[23]
His form joined the mist,
and he was lost from sight.
(circling right, goes to shite spot, and after facing front, exits down bridge)

---

[21]*Mukashi otoko*, the popular epithet for Narihira derived from a number of episodes in the *Tales of Ise* beginning, *mukashi otoko*, "Long ago, a man..."

[22]*Wa ga na o nan to yūbae no: yū* means both "evening" and "says" or "is called". In the translation, the "even if" is meant to suggest both the dilemma of naming as well as evening.

[23]*Harasan to yūbe no hitokasumi: Yū* again means both "evening" and "says," thus: *harasan to iu:* "will probably clear up, he says," and *yūbe no hitokasumi:* "fine mist of evening."

INTERLUDE

(The kyōgen, a person from Kitayamabe, comes out to the shite spot saying he is going to view the blossoms of the Unrin Temple. He goes to the corner and spots the waki. Prompted by questions from the waki, the kyōgen positions himself at stage center relates a little bit about Ariwara no Narihira's background, and then explains several theories concerning the authorship of the Tales of Ise. Recommending to the waki that he spend the night beneath the cherry tree, the kyōgen steps back to the kyōgen spot. Stage attendants remove the cherry tree prop.)

ACT TWO
(newer version; the older version follows)

ageuta	*(sitting at waki spot)*
WAKI &	And so we rest beneath the tree
WAKIZURE	silhouetted by the moon
	we rest beneath the tree
	silhouetted by the moon,
	the robe of blossoms
	that would "cloak me when evening falls"[24]
	I spread my sleeves and sleep
	I spread my sleeves and sleep.

issei music *(The shite enters, dressed wearing a middle-aged man's mask with a colored headband and a cap. He has on broad divided skirts with a strong pattern and an unlined hunting cloak.)*

genoei	*(goes to shite spot)*
SHITE	"Is not that the moon?
	Is this not the spring of old?
	Is it only my body
	which remains as it was?"[25]

kakeai	*(remains at waki spot)*
WAKI	How strange! A personage from the court appears, his magnificence reflected in the blossoms. What manner of person are you?

[24]Based on *Kokinshū* poem 95 by Sosei.

[25]*Kokinshū* poem 747 by Narihira; it also appears in *Tales of Ise* episode 4.

SHITE   What point is there in mystery now? I have come to tell you
             of the former days of "the man of old."

WAKI   If this is so, please disclose the secret of the *Tales of Ise* to
             me within this dream.

SHITE   As I begin my tale
             the blossom filled storm adds its voice

WAKI   to these secrets

SHITE   I reveal.
             (takes one step toward waki)

kuri   *(moves to center back stage)*
SHITE   Surely, it has often been asked what kind of people are those
             in the tale and why

CHORUS   were they so imbued with the dew of love,
             and it is right that the readers wonder this.[26]

sashi
SHITE   First of all, concealing themselves from the eyes of others,
             deep within the ladies' chambers[27]

CHORUS   as the lady lingered behind the screens, lost within her own
             reveries, my heart too, was stained with this flower, and to-
             gether a longing grew within us.
             (takes one step toward waki)

---

[26]These two lines are based on a sentence in the *Waka chikenshū,* a commentary on the
Tales of Ise by Minamoto Tsunenobu (1016-97). This text apparently made a deep impression
on Zeami, as either direct quotations from it or other evidence of its influence can be found in
the play *Izutsu* and in his treatise on musical types *Go on* (c.1430). It also appears in the play
Kakitsubata (Yokomichi and Omote 1960-63: 1, 438, n. 85.) This text is found in Katagiri 1969:
197-286.

[27]Allusion to the "Hana no En" chapter of the *Tale of Genji* associating the romantic
proclivities of Genji with those of Narihira, particularly the Narihira-Kōshi affair with the Genji-
Oborozuki affair (Yokomichi and Omote 1960-63: 1, 155, n.22; Sanari 1930-31: 468). Kōshi was
a niece of the Empress of the Fifth Ward and promised to the Emperor Seiwa; Oborozuki was a
sister of the reigning Empress (Kōkiden) and the intended of the Crown Prince. The Unrin
Temple is also the grave site of Murasaki Shikibu, the author of the *Tale of Genji.*

kuse　　　　　*(dances to the chorus' song)*
It is the second month
still evening yet
the moon is sinking
while we set out
on the paths of love!
(stamps)
Truly those places of renown
(moves to stage front)
mentioned in the tale
are within the palace grounds.[28]
(steps slightly to the left)
As I cross the Akuta River[29]
(moves to stage front)
I think of blossoms falling
layer upon layer
(looks around and stamps)
and, as Bishop Henjo has written,
"without realizing it, I lose my way."[30]
(moves to corner)
The robe covering her head
is the color of autumn leaves;[31]
(circles left to back center stage)

[28]Refers to a popular theory in classical scholarship that places cited in the *Tales of Ise* were actually places in the court itself. This theory is found in the *Waka chikenshū* and the text known as the *Reizeiryū Ise monogatari shō*. The former text seems aesthetically and philosophically closer to Zeami in its extensive use of Buddhist terminology and concepts to explain poetry; the Reizei text is rather sinocentric, liberally citing Chinese histories and Po Chü-i even in its explications of individual episodes of the *Tales of Ise*. The *Reizeiryū* text is in Katagiri 1969: 287-400.

[29]The Akuta River is mentioned in the *Tales of Ise* 6, the episode central to the older version of this play. As there is not as actual river in the vicinity with this name, many of the commentaries advance theories as to what river is actually being referred to. The *Waka chikenshū* suggests the Omiya River, while the *Reizeiryū Ise monogatari shō* favors the Hori River, a waterway used for refuse (*akuta*) disposal (Katagiri 1969: 232-3, 301). For a discussion of the proliferation of theories regarding the "real" identity of Akuta River see Moritomo 1969: 138-39.

[30]Based on *Kokinshū* poem 435 by Bishop Henjō, one of the six poetic geniuses, and founder of the Genkei Temple, of which the Unrin Temple was a branch. The *Waka chikenshū* cites this poem as proof that "Akuta" was an alternative name of the Ōmiya River, interpreting the word *akuta*, "garbage" in the poem, as a hidden reference to the Omiya River (Katagiri 1969: 234).

[31]*Momijigasane*: a color combination in which the outer garments are crimson and the inner ones green.

she walks her scarlet hakama
into disarray.
The sincere man[32]
who beckons her forward
(advances to stage center)
wears wisteria hakama,
a bit of the Murasaki plant.[33]
He lifts his dampened hem.
(with left hand, pulls the cuff cord up)

SHITE   *(opens fan)*
               Ah! The roads of Shinano![34]

CHORUS   His hunting cloak,
               the dark green of the horsetails
               so lush in Sonohara,
               (moves to stage front)
               he hoods himself with his sleeve
               (covers head with left sleeve)
               and steals away
               the evening moon of the second month, too
               (hides face with fan, circles right)
               is already departing.
               (stops at shite spot)
               Is that which falls through
               the hazy evening
               (goes to corner)
               the spring rain
               (looks up at sky)

---

[32]*Mame otoko*: another popular epithet for Narihira.

[33]Reference to Kokinshū poem 867 and a poem from the "Kiritsubo" chapter of the *Tale of Genji*. The roots of the *murasaki* (purple) plant were used to make a purple dye. *Murasaki* suggests a relationship and at times a semi-supernatural affinity between two people, which reinforces the imagistic association among *murasaki*, *iro* (passion/color) and *fuji* (wisteria). These allusions also serve to create links between the romance of Narihira and the Empress of the Second Ward and the romances of Genji, and literary parallels between the various works involved. *Murasaki* is important in the play *Kakitsubata*.

[34]Shinano acts as a *jo* or preface association for "dark green" (*tokusa iro*) in the chorus' line following (Yokomichi and Omote 1960-63: 1,156). *Tokusa*, "scouring rush," was a kind of horsetail, particularly abundant in Shinano. There is a poem about Shinano in the *Tales of Ise*, episode 8 which has no relevance to the present version of this play. It is alluded to in *Kakitsubata*.

or is it my tears,[35] he asks,
(looks down)
and drying his face with his sleeve,
he tucks up his robes
and departs forlorn,
wandering who knows where.
(circles left to back stage center)

ei   *(faces front)*
SHITE   I recall
                    the melody of an evening dance

CHORUS   *(goes to shite spot)*
                    as I turn back[36]
                    my sleeves
                    does the moon remember?

jonomai (The shite performs a long dance to instrumental music. It is danced slowly and with elegance.)

noriji
CHORUS   The evening's dance transforms the time
                    time passes in the evening's dance
                    (goes to center stage)
                    The moon that's left us[37]
                    lingers over the ravine
                    (lifts fan high)
                    the vision of the dream
                    from your boxwood pillow[38]
                    (circles to shite spot)

---

[35]Based on *Kokinshū* poem 88 by Ōtomo Kuronushi, another one of the six poetic geniuses.

[36]"Turn back," refers both to "turning back" the sleeves and "turning back" to the past.

[37]*Nagori no tsuki*: "the dawn moon" or "the waning moon." The word *nagori* is rich in nuances in classical Japanese, for example: "the traces of something after it is gone," "memories of the dead or of the past," "that which has remained in the heart after something has vanished," etc. The phrase first occurred in this play in the first *sageuta*. This repetition deepens its meaning, a typical phenomenon in noh.

[38]*Yume no tsuge no makura*: *tsuge* means both "revelation" and "boxwood." Thus *yume no tsuge*: "revelation in the dream," and *tsuge no makura*: "boxwood pillow."

returns me to my dancer's robe,
splashed with mountain indigo.
There is no telling this tale to an end.
(faces waki; goes to sit at center stage)

SHITE   The needles of the pine tree
               never become scattered and lost,[39]

CHORUS   the needles of the pine
               never become scattered and lost
               (the shite stands, stamps)
               In the generations to come
               they will know of this love
               there will be evenings to tell
               of the *Tales of Ise,*
               (faces the waki)
               of the past that leaves
               its words like grasses cut
               of a moment, and as tender.[40]
               The evening which brought forth
               this tale is no longer--
               Was it a dream from which I have awakened?
               It is a dream from which I have awakened.
               (flips sleeve over arm and stamps to end the play)

ACT TWO
(older version of the play)

(In this version, there is a structure representing a grave mound covered with cloth at back center stage. At the opening of the second act, the cloth is removed, revealing a beautiful woman sitting within it. The stage directions are the suppositions of the Japanese editors.)

[39]Based on a phrase in the Japanese preface to the *Kokinshū*, describing the editor's wishes for the longevity of the collection. By analogy, this phrase refers to the *Tales of Ise* here.

[40]There is an elaborate play in this section on *koto no ha*: "leaves (or needles) of speech" or "word, language." The phrase reverberates with the opening line of the Japanese preface to the *Kokinshū*: "Japanese poetry is that which takes the human heart as its seed and grows forth as the myriad leaves of speech."

kakeai
WAKI   How wondrous! Beneath the blossoms in the deepening
              night, a splendid maiden appears in purple robes and scarlet
              trousers. Who might you be?

TSURE   I am ashamed to confess that in the past I was known as the
              Empress of the Second Ward. Because of karmic chains I
              have returned, as blossoms to their roots or birds to their old
              nests.[41]

WAKI   Am I really hearing this?
              Are you the Empress of the Second Ward?
              If so, please reveal to me
              the secrets of the *Tales of Ise*.

TSURE   As I begin my tale of the past
              the blossom-filled storm adds its voice
              to these secrets I reveal.
              (takes one step toward waki)

kuri   *(The tsure emerges from the mound and stands stage center.)*
CHORUS   Surely, it has often been asked what kind of people are those
              in the tale and why
              were they so imbued with the dew of love,
              and it is right that the readers wonder this.[42]

sashi   *(motionless)*
TSURE   First of all, it is written
              "Musashi Plain,"
              and yet the grasses of Kasuga field
              are a young green[43]

CHORUS   changing the colors, plucking the flowers--what becomes of
              the meaning?

---

[41]Based on a poem by Retired Emperor Sutoku (1119-64), in the *Senzaishū*, the seventh
imperial anthology.

[42]See note 26 above.

[43]Poem number 17 in the *Kokinshū* begins with the line *Kusagano wa*; however, the same
poem appears in the *Tales of Ise* episode 12, with the first line *Musashino wa*. The poem is
quoted in the *jōnoei* below. This discrepancy contributed to the medieval theories about the deliberate codification of place names in the text (Yokomichi and Omote 1960, 1: 438, n. 86).
Green is mentioned for its association with "color" in the next line.

Truly, truly, who can decide
Between Ise and Hyūga?[44]

sageuta   *(tsure moves slightly)*
CHORUS   That which is called
the Grave of Musashi Plain
Is in truth within Kasuga Field.
Thus in Kasuga Field with time
as short as the spaces
between the antlers of a stag[45]
in a raised voice
I recited this poem

jōnoei   *(stamps rhythmically)*
CHORUS   "Musashi Plain
do not set it aflame today
tender as the young grasses
my spouse is hidden here
I too lie hidden"[46]

deha entrance music *(The tsure goes to back corner and sits down. The shite enters, probably wearing broad divided skirts with a strong pattern with a large cloak and tossing his mane of black hair.)*

sashi   *(stopping at first pine)*
SHITE   I am the ghost of Mototsune, the elder brother of the Empress. Seeking to reveal to you the secrets of the *Tales of Ise* within this dream, the Empress too has appeared here, a place with ties to the *Tales of Ise*.
Musashi Plain--do not set it aflame today--The spouse as tender as young grasses

[44]"Ise and Hyūga" are the two place which the *shidai* of *Unoha* declare are similar, see note 1 to that translation for an explanation of their relationship. The *Waka chikenshū* cites a folk tale about the two places and explains their significance: after one man from each place died on the same day, it was discovered that the Ise man had died before his time. As his body had already been cremated, the Ise man's soul returned to the body of the Hyūga man, who had been buried. When the combined body and soul returned to life, great confusion ensued among the two wives and sets of children. Thus "Ise and Hyūga" came to mean reversals and confusions and therefore describes the reversals of time and place which occur in the *Tales of Ise* (Yokomichi and Omote 1960-63: 1, 438-39, n. 87).

[45]From *Shinkokinshū* poem 1273 by Kakinomoto no Hitomaro. A different version of his poem found in *Manyōshū* IV, 502.

[46]This is the poem referred to in note 43 above.

was Narihira,
the poet was the Empress,
he who took her back was I, Mototsune,
appearing to you in the figure
of the "one gulp demon"[47]
is this devil's form
originally Mototsune--

issei SHITE	*(entering stage)* can I, in this unstable form

CHORUS   Narihira's past into the present?[48]

genoei
SHITE
(standing at shite spot)
Do you recall the past when you asked
"What is that white gem?"
as night sped towards morn?

kakeai
TSURE
(going to center stage)
When I think of the
"my fault" shrimp that lives within
the seaweed the fishermen glean[49]
I do not blame the world.

SHITE
Then the bitterness forgetting grasses[50]
now even this evening make manifest
(faces tsure)
the tale retreating on the path of dreams
and reveal it to this traveler.

[47]This is the demon who caused the death of the woman (presumably Kōshi) who asked what the dew drop was in the *Tales of Ise* episode 6. See the question about the "white gem" in the genoei below and note 17 to the Unoha translation above.

[48]The text plays on the names Mototsune and Narihira. *Moto* means "originally" and *tsune* is repeated in the phrase *tsune naki*, "unstable." *Nari* pivots to mean "become." In the translation the pivot is "form," which is used as a noun in the shite's line and a verb in conjunction with the chorus' line.

[49]From *Kokinshū* poem 807 by Fujiwara Naoiko; *warekara* is the name of a shrimp, but also means "from myself." The poem also appears in the *Tales of Ise* episode 65, a tale about Ariwara and the empress.

[50]*Wasuregusa*: a type of grass, *wasure* is the stem of the verb meaning "forget." An allusion to anonymous poem 766 of the *Kokinshū*.

TSURE	Having passed the years, forgotten determined that the past be seen by no one we flee into Musashi Plain. *(goes to corner)*
SHITE	Though they say Musashi Plain is without limit, is it not bound by the path of love? *(goes to center stage and looks at tsure)* How long hidden lover
TSURE	fleeing into the Musashi Mound where the past too lies hidden[51] *(enters tomb and sits down)*
SHITE	In truth, you have appeared here, and yet behind you *(goes to corner and looks around)* the shadows gather without end *(circles left to shite spot)* darkness upon darkness what is to be done? *(takes pine torch from stage attendant)*
uta SHITE	*(stamps)* Setting fire to this field
CHORUS	setting fire to this field as the bird catchers do we search *(goes toward prop)* and find a lone grave mound and within, how uncanny, he says
SHITE	Brandishing the pine torch
CHORUS	brandishing the pine torch we enter the grave tomb and so indeed

[51]Because the tsure (Kōshi) is in the structure representing the grave mound in Musashi where she had hidden when she fled with Narihira, this line could also mean, "where I lay hidden in the past too" or even "where others (before me) had hidden themselves in the past" (Yokomichi & Omote 1960-63: 1, n. 90.

(raises torch and looks at tsure)
the Empress is within.
(faces front)
Truly, the sincere man
deserves the fame he has.
What a wretched thing
(stamps)
is worldly renown
Look, the Empress is in agony
(turns toward the tsure)

rongi   *(During this the tsure goes to the waki spot and sits beside waki.)*

CHORUS   "Passing the years
living in this hamlet
if I were to depart,
living in this hamlet
if I were to depart,
like its name, Deep Grasses
would Fukakusa become
a wild field?"[52]
Thinking of the world long gone
I fall into shame.
(shite looks down)

SHITE   "If it became a wild field
I would become a quail
and call to you,
I would become a quail
and call to you,
from time to time
might you not come hunting?"[53]
Even this, her loving response
evokes pity

CHORUS   Truly from my heart
this is bitter[54]

[52]Poem 971 in the *Kokinshū* by Narihira; it also appears in the *Tales of Ise* episode 123.

[53]The response to the previous poem in both the *Kokinshū* (972) and the *Tales of Ise* (123). *Kari* means both "occasionally" or "sporadically" and "to hunt."

[54]The *kara* of *karakoromo* (Chinese robe, in the following line) also means "bitter."

"like the Chinese robe
grown so familiar with wear
because I have a wife

SHITE   this road on which
I have come so far"[55]
brings longing thoughts of her.
How painful climbing Mount Utsu[56]

CHORUS   am I awake or within a dream
as I travel, travel.
Oh capital bird
on the shores of the Sumida River

SHITE   Let me ask[57]
is Musashi Plain

CHORUS   truly in the East?

SHITE   or is it perhaps the Capital?

CHORUS   It is in truth Kasuga,
it is in truth Kasuga
"field guard, by the signal fires of Tobuhi
venture out and look!"[58]
above is Mt. Mikasa,
and in the foothills
Kasuga Plain

[55]The first four lines of the "iris" poem from *Ise monogatari* 9 (also *Kokinshū* poem 410 by Narihira). The first syllable in each line spells out *kakitsubata* (iris). For further analysis see the notes to the play *Kakitsubata* in this volume.

[56]This and the references to the capital bird continue the allusions to *Ise monogatari* episode 9 which began with the Chinese cloak. Mt. Utsu suggests the word *utsutsu* (waking state) in the next line.

[57]In the *Tales of Ise* 9 the capital bird is asked if the poet's beloved is still alive. The question posed here relates to the theory that the place names in the tale actually refer to places in the capital.

[58]Lines from anonymous *Kokinshū* poem 18 (sometimes numbered 19) which asks the guard to see how long before the young herbs will be ready to pick. Tobuhino is a section of Kasuga, but *tobuhi* were signal fires used for their smoke in the day and their flames at night. This meaning gave rise to the practice of using it with the word *nomori* (field guardian) whether or not he was at Kasuga.

where the stags's mate lies hidden.
In the end I retrieved the Empress
from this grave mound in Musashi
and thinking to return...
The dawn breaks,
gazing around
it is neither Musashi nor Kasuga
but the capital
at the Unrin Temple
in Murasaki Field
beneath the blossoms,
at the Unrin temple
beneath the blossoms
Mototsune[59] and the Empress'
appearance has become a dream
everything has become a dream.

[59]The *moto* of Mototsune also means beneath--*hana no moto*: "beneath the blossoms."

KAKITSUBATA 杜若

translated by Susan Blakeley Klein

CHARACTERS

Waki: A traveling priest

Shite: The spirit of the kakitsubata iris

SETTING: A summer day at Eight Bridges in Mikawa. The time is uncertain.

AUTHOR: Traditionally attributed to Zeami. Itō Masayoshi postulates Zenchiku as the most likely author.

CATEGORY: A third category, woman play. The stick drum is used.

PERFORMANCE PRACTICES: Performed by all schools with a wide variety of variant performances.

TEXTS: The translation is based on Itō, 1983-86: 1, 257-266, 422-424. Most of the references to the *Tales of Ise* commentaries come from Itō's notes. Some of the movement descriptions are from the translator's notes taken at recent performances.

SOURCES: The *Tales of Ise* and commentaries on that work.

TRANSLATIONS: English, Pound 1917, Sadler 1934, Shimazaki 1972-81; French, Sieffert 1979.

KAKITSUBATA (The Iris)

Translated by Susan Blakeley Klein

A PLAY IN ONE ACT

nanori music   (The waki, a travelling priest, enters wearing a wide-sleeved, travelling cloak of plain weave over a small-sleeved, silk kimono and a priest's head covering. He carries a rosary. When he reaches the shite spot he faces forward.)

nanori WAKI	*(facing front)* I am a monk, taking a look at the various provinces. Not too long ago I was in the capital and while there I left no famous spot or historical site unseen. Now I have set my heart on a pilgrimage to the Eastern provinces.
ageuta WAKI	Night after night on pillows transient, night after night on pillows transient, *(takes a few steps to indicate travel)* the lodgings diverse and oft-changing, yet the same body, fated to drift in uneasy slumber--Mino, Owari,[1] Mikawa at last, I've arrived, Mikawa at last, I've arrived.[2]
tsukizerifu WAKI	I have travelled so quickly that in no time at all I have reached Mikawa, land of "Three Rivers." *(looks down)* Here along the edge of the marsh I see the kakitsubata iris are just now in full bloom. *(goes toward center front)* I believe I'll go a bit closer to take a better look.

---

[1] *Ukine no mi no owari: ukine* can mean both "sad sleep" and "floating weed;" *mi no owari* indicates both "the body's end" or "one's fate" and "Mino, Owari" two provinces in what are now Gifu and Aichi prefectures.

[2] Mikawa (Three Rivers) is in the eastern part of present day Aichi prefecture.

66

sashi   *(facing front)*
WAKI   Truly, time never tarries:
spring slips by, summer's at hand;
the artless trees and grass mind not,
we say, yet mindful of the season
these flowers arrayed in color--
are they not also called "sweet faces"?
Ah, these kakitsubata are so beautiful!
(goes to waki spot)

yobikake   *(The shite calls to the waki from beyond the partially raised curtain, and then enters dressed as a local woman in the young woman mask, a brocade robe in bright colors worn straight over an inner kimono of white satin with gold or silver patterning.)*
SHITE   You there, holy man, may I ask what it is that keeps you lingering by that marsh?

mondō   *(turning to face the shite)*
WAKI   I am merely a man taking a look at the various provinces, and I have paused here fascinated by the splendor of these kakitsubata. Could you tell me the name of this place?

SHITE   *(crossing the bridge toward the stage)*
Actually, this is Mikawa's famed "Eight Bridges,"
a place well known for its kakitsubata.
(halts)
Naturally, the flowers that make this place famous
(faces front)
are dyed a purple one shade deeper
than ordinary flowers, to which
they must not be compared;[3]
these kakitsubata alone deserve
your special attention,
as you would know if you were a

---

[3]*Murasaki,* the color purple as well as the plant used to make purple dye, conventionally stands for relationships because of poem 867 in the *Kokinshū*: "Because of that single stalk of purple, all the other grasses on the plain of Musashi seem much more dear." Here, however, the usual association is being denied: because the kakitsubata's purple color is so deep, it is not to be thought of as related to ordinary flowers. The word for color, *iro,* also means passion, and *murasaki* can be a metaphor for wife. Consequently "deep purple color" may also imply a "deeply passionate wife."

<blockquote>
traveller of any sensitivity!
(shite moves forward)
</blockquote>

WAKI

<blockquote>
Ah, yes--it seems to me the
kakitsubata of Eight Bridges in Mikawa
were sung of in an old poem.
What poet's words were they,
could you tell me?
</blockquote>

SHITE

<blockquote>
(reaches shite spot, turns to face waki)
According to the *Tales of Ise*,
this place has come to be called
Eight Bridges
because here the stream, spreading
its spider legs, is spanned eight-fold.
Noticing that in this marsh
kakitsubata were blooming
in magnificent disarray, someone suggested,
"Let's compose poems on the topic
'Spirit of Travel,'
beginning each line with a syllable
from the word kakitsubata."[4]
"Rare robe of Cathay--
its hem from long wearing worn
once by my wife when we were close
how far, far from her
I've wandered."
Thus Ariwara no Narihira[5]
composed a poem about these kakitsubata.
</blockquote>

kakeai
WAKI

<blockquote>
(waki turns to face shite)
Ah, how interesting!
</blockquote>

---

[4]The story and poem are taken from the *Tales of Ise*, episode 9. Each of the five lines in the Japanese acrostic begins with a syllable from *kakitsubata*: *karakoromo kitsutsu narenishi tsuma shi areba harubaru kinuru tabi o shizo omou*. The pillow word *karakoromo*, here translated as "rare robe of Cathay," originally meant a robe from China and therefore connoted rare elegance. There are three puns: *tsuma* means "wife" and "robe hem"; *nare* means "become familiar, intimate with" and "become soft from wearing"; and *ki* means "to wear" and "to come." For a fuller analysis of the poem see McCullough 1968: 203-204.

[5]Ariwara no Narihira (825-880) was a famous poet, who became a much romanticized figure largely because he was popularly identified as the hero of most of the *Tales of Ise* episodes. In episode 9 he leaves the capital presumably in disgrace after having attempted to abduct his illicit lover Fujiwara Kōshi (842-910), who later became the consort of Emperor Seiwa.

You mean Narihira travelled
down east even as far
as these remote provinces?

SHITE   *(facing the waki)*
At last you've asked something worthwhile!
Not only to these Eight Bridges,
still deeper into the heart
of the North he travelled[6]
from one famed spot to another
along the road

WAKI   to places in various provinces;
yet to the end, his heart
with special longing yearned

SHITE   to cross the long span of years back
to these Eight Bridges hung over[7]

WAKI   the marsh of kakitsubata in Mikawa.

SHITE   "How far, far from her!"

WAKI   he wonders,[8] passion-stained
thoughts lingering even as

SHITE   Narihira,[9] the lover, fades into the past;

---

[6]*Kokoro no oku fukaki* means both "deep into the heart(land) of the North" and "with a deeply hidden heart." The latter reading hints that Narihira's travels had deeper allegorical meaning. According to the *Tales of Ise,* episodes 14 and 15, Narihira travelled on to Michinoku after leaving Eight Bridges.

[7]*Toriwaki kokoro no sue kakete omoiwatarishi yatsuhashi*: puns on *kakete* meaning "to hang (one's heart on)" and, in relation to the bridge, "to span"; and *watarishi*, "(to think about) over a long period of time" and "to cross (the bridge)."

[8]The last two lines of the *karakoromo* poem. *Omou* has been changed to *omoi* in order to create a pivot into *omoi no iro* (the color of passionate thoughts/yearning). The underlying meaning here is that traces of Narihira's passionate thoughts have been left behind in the world, and are manifested in the color of the kakitsubata that remain as his memento.

[9]This is the first of two pivots on Ariwara no Narihira's name in this section. Here, Narihira pivots on *nari* (become): *nushi wa mukashi ni nari/hira* (Narihira, the lover, has become part of the past).

WAKI	these flowers a memento
SHITE	*(turning towards front)* here and now
ageuta CHORUS	*(slowly circles the stage as chorus sings)* remain as Ariwara's traces,[10] don't veil from view this fence of iris[11] don't veil from view this fence of iris. The water at the marsh edge is not shallow, nor were the vows of the man, his thoughts divided as this spider-legged bridge.[12] Even now, while to the traveler the old tale is told, the day's end draws closer hearts worn soft and fond, draws closer hearts worn soft and fond.
mondō SHITE	*(facing the waki)* I have something I would like to ask of you.
WAKI	*(turns to face shite)* What might that be?
SHITE	Although it's very humble, I invite you to pass the night in my hut.
WAKI	With pleasure. I'll follow presently. *(waki goes to the waki spot and kneels)*

ashirai music *(The shite goes to the koken spot and kneels facing the back panel. The stage attendants remove the brocade robe and replace it with a three-quarter length dancing cloak of gauze weave. A hat is placed on the shite's head, and an*

[10]*Katami no hana wa ima koko ni ari/wara no ato*: here the pivot is on the verb "to be" (*ari*) in Ariwara: "the flower mementos here and now are/Ariwara's traces."

[11]*Ato na hedate so kakitsubata*: *hedate* (to screen off, stand between, estrange) is related to *kaki* (fence) hidden in kakitsubata. This line can be taken to mean, "Don't neglect these kakitsubata, which are Ariwara's mementos."

[12]This simile of Narihira's divided thoughts points to the interpretation given in the *Reizeiryu Ise monogatari shō* (the Reizei commentary on Ise monogatari) that Eight Bridges stood for the eight women that Narihira could never bring himself to abandon, and Mikawa (Three Rivers) represented his three true loves.

ornate sword is attached to his side. The shite takes a fan and stands at the shite spot.)

mondō	*(spreading her right and left sleeves wide)*
SHITE	Pray look at this court cap and Chinese robe!
WAKI	*(still kneeling)*
	How strange! From out the doorway
	of that rough dwelling you come,
	wearing a robe of radiant color
	and a young man's court cap,
	saying, "Look at these!"
	What can this mean?
SHITE	This is none other than the robe of
	Cathay written of in the poem:
	the rare robe of Empress Takako.[13]
	As for the court cap, Narihira
	wore it at the autumn *gosechi*
	dance for an abundant harvest.[14]
	These mementos, the cap and robe,
	I keep close beside me and cherish.
WAKI	Leaving aside the cap and robe for the moment, tell me what
	manner of being you really are.
SHITE	In truth,
	I am the spirit of the kakitsubata:
	"left planted by the house of old a fence
	of iris..." so goes a poem
	whose words reveal
	a woman into an iris transformed;[15]

[13]Takako is another reading for Koshi, the woman Narihira attempted to run away with. See note 5 above.

[14]The *gosechi* dances were performed at the imperial banquet after the autumn harvest ceremony. Although usually performed by young girls, a medieval commentary, *Ise monogatari nangichū,* claims that Narihira was one of the dancers. This explains how the sheltered Takako came to be attracted to him.

[15]*Ueokishi mukashi no yado no kakitsubata:* the quote is a variation on the first three lines of *Gosenshū* 160 by Yoshimine no Yoshikata (d. 947): *Iisomeshi mukashi no yado no kakitsubata iro bakari koso katami narikere,* "Our first meeting at that house of old: the fence of iris, its color alone remains as a reminder". There is a reply poem in *Setsugyokushū* (a personal poetry collec-

and Narihira, as the heavenly
Bodhisattva of Song and Dance
become mortal,[16]
leaves inscribed in sheaves of poetry
miraculous sermons
on the Buddha's body of law.
When drenched in these dew-like
blessings, even trees and grasses
bear forth in fruitful enlightenment.[17]

kakeai   *(turning to face the shite)*
WAKI   To find such a miracle in this
              degenerate world! It appears
              that I have been exchanging words
              of holy law with an insentient being.

SHITE   Performing a Buddhist rite
              the dancing form of
              Narihira, the Man of Old[18]

WAKI   is indeed the
              Bodhisattva of Song and Dance

SHITE   *(turning to waki)*
              temporarily made mortal, Narihira[19]

---

tion by Sanjōnishi Sanekata, 1455-1537): *Mukashi no iro ni idezu wa sore to miji itodo hedatsuru yado no mukashi o.* "If this purple color no longer bloomed forth, you'd not remember, and more and more estranged from the house of old you'd become." A note states the woman became a kakitsubata.

[16]*Kabu no bosatsu:* according to a commentary on the *Tales of Ise,* the *Waka chikenshū,* traditionally attributed to Minamoto Tsunenobo (1016-97), Narihira was a Bodhisattva of Song and Dance, as well as an incarnation of the horse-headed Kannon.

[17]Here I've emphasized the conventional associations of *koto-no-ha* (word-leaf), which include "trees and grasses," "the dew of mercy," and "the Buddhist fruit" i.e., enlightenment. A more complete translation might be: "Because Narihira was a manifestation of the Bodhisattva of Song and Dance, even the poems that he composed and left behind for us are all miraculous sermons of the Buddha's body of laws; their efficacy is such that when they are intoned as prayers the dew-like blessings of Buddha's enlightenment reach even as far as insentient trees and grasses."

[18]As the hero of the *Tales of Ise,* Narihira is referred to as *mukashi otoko,* "the Man of Old."

[19]There is another pun on Narihira's name: *nari* is used in its meaning of "become, made."

WAKI	left Buddha's Capital of Tranquil Light
SHITE	to bring salvation and
WAKI	blessings to all
SHITE	along the path

shidai CHORUS	*(facing front)* far, far he wandered in way-worn Cathay robe far, far he wandered in way-worn Cathay robe I wear now, that I might dance.

issei SHITE	*(standing at shite spot)* Separation and after, traces of bitterness seen lining a Chinese robe,[20]
CHORUS	its dancing sleeves towards the capital with longing turn.

iroe dance *(a circling of the stage to instrumental music. The shite ends the dance in front of the drums.)*

kuri SHITE	Now as to this story it relates who it was and why[21]
CHORUS	his thoughts tearful as the dew on Moss Fern Mountain[22]

---

[20]*Wakarekoshi ato no urami no karakoromo: ato* means both "afterwards" and "traces." *Urami* means "bitterness, regret," while *ura* refers to the robe's lining and *mi* means "to see."

[21]This introductory phrase is based in part on a phrase from the *Waka chikenshū*. It is also used in the *kuri* section of *Unrin'in*.

[22]*Shinobu yama*, translated here as "Moss Fern Mountain," is in Fukushima prefecture. *Shinobu* can also mean "to do secretly, or conceal," and "recollect, cherish the memory of." Here it is written with characters meaning "faithful spouse." An alternative translation of this section might be: "with hidden tears I cherish the memory of a faithful spouse, as I travel this mountain road (i.e. life) that has no beginning or end." There is an allusion to a poem found in the *Tales of Ise*, episode 15: *shinobuyama shinobite kayō michi mo gana hito no kokoro no oku*

secretly travelled along this
grassy path that has no beginning or end.

sashi   *(facing front)*
SHITE   Once, the Man of Old, having
taken on the cap of manhood
in the old capital of Nara,
went hunting on his estate
near the village of "Spring Day."[23]

CHORUS   It must have been in the reign of Ninmyo,
whose most auspicious order he received[24]
as the spring mists rose round the palace
at the beginning of the third month
so he rose in imperial favor;
sent as envoy to the Spring Day festival
he was permitted the elegant court cap

SHITE   by the deep generosity of the Emperor

CHORU   She had his coming of age ceremony
at court, a rare occurrence indeed;
perhaps that's why it is
(figure-eight fan to express emotion)
called "the coming of age hat."

kuse   *(dances during this segment)*[25]
CHORUS   However, in this life a man's path
may at one time prosper
at another time, decline--

mo mirubeku, "Would there were a way to travel unobserved, secret as Mount Shinobu's name, for then your innermost heart I should see" (McCullough 1968: 80, 208).

[23]The opening lines of the first episode of the *Tales of Ise,* Teika version. *Ui-kamuri,* "the cap of manhood" refers to the coming-of-age ceremony for boys between the ages of 10 and 15. Kasuga (Spring Day) village was probably at the foot of Mount Kasuga in Nara (Vos 1957, II: 65).

[24] Emperor Ninmyō reigned from 833 through 850. These lines are based on the *Reizeiryū Ise monogatari shō.*

[25]This is a double *kuse (nidanguse),* and as such it contains two lines sung by the shite. The double kuse, which also occurs in *Genjikuyō,* probably derived from performances by *kuse-mai* dancers whose art Kan'ami learned. Many plays which contain a double kuse, i.e. *Yamamba* and *Hyakuman*, are indeed about dancers.

(stamps)
this principle held true
for Narihira's fate.
(moving towards center stage)
In search of a place to live,
eastward he drifted like the
clouds to Ise and Owari,
where he watched the waves
(sweeping point to look at sea)
rise on the sea:
(makes a big circle around the stage)
"My love for one left
further and further behind
deepens my envy for
these waves that homeward turn."[26]
(reaches spot in front of drums)
Reciting thus to himself,
he travelled on till Shinano's
Asama Peak he reached.
(goes forward to look off into the distance)
In the evening glow he saw
the billowing smoke;

SHITE   *(raising open fan)*
         "From Asama Peak in Shinano,
         smoke spirals upward.

CHORUS   People near and far,
         can they see it without awe?"[27]
         (stamps)
         he recited.
         Still further in way-worn robe travelling[28]
         (zigzag to center front)
         he reached Mikawa;
         here, the famous Eight Bridges,
         (pointing downward)

---

[26]A variation on a poem in the *Tales of Ise*, episode 7. In the noh version, *sugiyuki* (passing by) is replaced by *suginishi* (left behind). The lines introducing the poem are a combination of the headnotes for episodes 7 and 8.

[27]Poem from the *Tales of Ise*, episode 8. Mount Asama is an active volcano on the border of Nagano and Gumma prefectures.

[28]*Nao harubaru no tabigoromo:* another reworking of the *karakoromo* poem.

fragrant iris along the marsh edge,
(circles the stage)
associating their deep purple
with his love, "How is she?"
(stamps)
wondered the man from the capital.
(points toward waki with left hand)
Among the many varied episodes
(moves towards center front)
found in this tale
the story of these Eight Bridges is
especially profound;
deep as Mikawa's waters are
fathomless and true the vows
(several stamps)
made to those women
whose names tell many a tale:
(circles the stage to right)
"the woman who waits for her love"[29]
"the love-sick one,"[30]
"the jeweled bamboo blind"[31]
(reaches shite spot, turns, goes forward)
its tangled light dancing fireflies
(points towards front and gazes up)
"high above the clouds
should you soar,
(flips sleeves, cloud fan)
tell the wild geese
that autumn breezes blow"[32]

---

[29]From the *Tales of Ise*, episode 17. *Waka chikenshū* took this episode to refer to Ki no Aritsune's daughter, who was supposed to have been Narihira's wife. In the *issei* section of the noh play *Izutsu*, the shite (Ki no Aritsune's daughter) identifies herself by this epithet.

[30]From the *Tales of Ise*, episode 45. See note 32 below.

[31]From episode 64. *Tama* (jewel) leads to *hikari* (light) which in turn leads to the fireflies.

[32]From a poem in episode 45 of the *Tales of Ise: yuku hotaru kumo no ue made inubeku akikaze fuku to kari ni tsugekose*, "flying fireflies, as you can go above the clouds, please tell the wild geese that the autumn breezes are blowing." The headnote claims that a man composed this after hearing that a young girl had died of unrequited love for him. The wild geese, who return to Japan in the autumn, are a metaphor for the girl, who has departed in the springtime of her life. The poem indicates Narihira's wish that she too might return again now that it is autumn.

(circles the stage)
fleetingly I appear
for all the earth's salvation.
"Are you aware or not,
that those of this world

SHITE   *(zigzag forward to center stage)*
unto darkness will not go"[33]
for the dawn's

CHORUS   *(stamps)*
all-enlightening "moon
is not the same--
nor is this spring,
the spring of old.
My body alone
remains unchanged"[34] as the
(changes fan to left hand)
embodiment of Absolute Reality,
(brings hands together, spreads them wide)
and the God of Harmonious Love[35]--
so Narihira is known;
(goes to shite spot and faces waki)
this tale I've told,
(feather fan, small circle right)
do not doubt it traveler.
Far, far he wandered in
way-worn Cathay robe
I wear now, that I might dance.
(stops back center stage facing forward)

[33]According to *Ise monogatari zuinō*, the poem alluded to here was composed by Narihira to comfort Ki no Aritsune's daughter as she lay weeping beside Narihira's deathbed: *shiru ya kimi ware ni narenuru yo no hito no kuraki ni yukanu tayori ari to wa*, "Do you know, my love, the saying, 'Be assured that those in the world who become intimate with me will not go unto darkness'?"

[34]Narihira's famous poem from the *Tales of Ise*, episode 4. For discussions of this poem in its original context see McCullough, *Brocade by Night*, pp. 211-12; McCullough, *Tales of Ise*, pp. 52-53; or Brower and Miner, pp. 193, 290, and 476.

[35]According to *Ise monogatari zuinō*, Narihira was the God of Yin-Yang (*innyō no kami*, here taken to mean harmonious conjugal love) whose goal was to help those caught in the trap of earthly passions.

uta
SHITE   "Among flowers flit butterflies
                     whirling flakes of snow

CHORUS   through willows skim warblers
                     flashing specks of gold"[36]

jonomai (*The shite performs a slow, graceful dance in three parts to the music of the flute, hand drums and stick drum.*)

waka   (*standing at shite spot with fan raised*)
SHITE   "left planted by the house of old
                     a fence of iris

CHORUS   (*zigzags forward and goes to corner*)
                     its color alone"
                     remains as of old[37]
                     its color alone
                     remains as of old
                     its color alone

wakauke
SHITE   retains the name of the Man of Old
                     which lingers also in
                     the flowering orange tree's[38]

noriji   fading fragrance, and mingles with[39]
                     a garland of sweetflag.

CHORUS   (*circles the stage and stops at center*)
                     Their hues, so alike--
                     which is which?

[36]A poem from the Chinese poetry collection *Hyakuren shōkai.*

[37]*Iro bakari koso mukashi narikere*: a variation on the last two lines of the poem mentioned in note 15 above.

[38]The Man of Old is associated with the flowering orange tree in the *Tales of Ise,* episode 60.

[39]These lines are an allusion to Ki no Tsurayuki's comment in the Japanese preface to the *Kokinshū*: "The poetry of Ariwara no Narihira tries to express too much content (*kokoro*) in too few words (*kotoba*). It resembles a faded flower with a lingering fragrance" (McCullough 1985: 7).

the kakitsubata and sweetflag's
color so deep
in the trees cries
(looks upwards, then downward to listen)

SHITE   the cicada, casting off
               its empty Cathay robe[40]
               (kneels, holds out left sleeve on fan and gazes at it)

CHORUS   for sleeves of dazzling white
               (stands and circles stage)
               deuzia blossoms, as snowy
               night lightens
               (cloud fan at center stage)
               to the east, dawn's
               glimmering clouds
               of pale purple[41]
               (flips sleeve and goes forward)
               kakitsubata
               whose heart of enlightenment
               (figure-eight fan)
               unfurls
               truly, in this moment
               (extends fan and circles stage)
               trees, grasses and all the earth
               truly, in this moment
               trees, grasses and all the earth
               acquire with her
               (faces forward at shite spot, flips sleeve)
               enlightenment's fruit
               (concluding stamps)
               and with this she vanishes.

[40]The cicada's empty shell (*kara*) was seen as a symbol of transience; here as the cicada sheds its shell, so the *kakitsubata* sheds her attachment to her dark purple color. The chorus emphasizes the change by listing a catalogue of white, bright images: dazzling white sleeves, deuzia blossoms, snow, and dawn's glimmering light.

[41]This mention of pale purple brings the list of white images to an end. Purple clouds are said to transport Amida Buddha as he comes to welcome souls to his Pure Land Paradise.

SAIGYŌZAKURA

西行櫻

translated by **Eileen Katō**

CHARACTERS

Waki:	The poet-priest Saigyō in old age
Wakizure: (tachishu)	A crowd of Kyoto flower viewers. One of them, the leader, speaks individually.
Shite:	The spirit of an old cherry tree
Kyōgen:	Saigyō's servant

SETTING: Afternoon and evening of a spring day toward the end of the 12th century, late in Saigyō's life (1118-1190). The place is Saigyō's Hermitage, here set in the Western Hills of Kyoto, though it was actually in the Eastern Hills.

AUTHOR: Zeami

CATEGORY: This play is one of four pieces without female characters which are nevertheless classified as pseudo, third-category, women plays. *Unrin'in* is another. It may also be categorized as a fourth-category, miscellaneous piece.

PERFORMANCE PRACTICES: Performed by all five schools.

TEXTS: Yokomichi and Omote 1960-63: 1, 287-294 was the basic text
                used, although Sanari 1930-31: 3, 1167-80 and Nogami 1971:
                3, 179-198 were also consulted. Stage directions are partly
                noted from recent performances.

SOURCES: A poem by Saigyō, and his comment that it was written when
                flower-viewers disturbed his quiet. In *Sankashū* and
                Gyokuyōshū.

NOTES: An attempt has been made to keep waka poems in 5-7 meter,
                even respecting the *jiamari* (extra syllable) in the last line of
                Saigyō's poem. The meter of the Chinese poems proved
                impossible to transpose directly into English.

SAIGYŌZAKURA (Saigyō and the Cherry Tree)

Translated by Eileen Katō

A PLAY IN ONE ACT

(After the musicians enter, two attendants bring on the stage prop, a covered wooden frame with a branch of flowering cherry stuck in it. The prop is set up at back center stage. The waki comes on without musical accompaniment and is followed by the kyōgen. The waki goes and sits on a stool at the waki spot. He is dressed in a travel cloak over white divided skirts; he has on a priest's hood and carries a Buddhist rosary. The kyōgen, a temple servant, wears a travel cloak over trousers and has on a servant's cap. He sits at the kyōgen spot.)

mondō

WAKI	Ho! Is there anyone there?
KYŌGEN	*(half rising)* Here I am, Sir.
WAKI	I have something on my mind. Let people know that cherry blossom viewing is forbidden this year at this hermitage.
KYŌGEN	Very well, Sir. I understand.

(Kyōgen rises, goes to the shite spot, and faces front.)

KYŌGEN	Oh me! Oh my! this is most awkward. The famous cherry tree that blossoms at this hermitage cannot be hidden from the world. Every year when spring comes round, flower-viewers flock here, high and low, rich and poor regardless, but this year--I have no idea why!--my master says flower viewing is forbidden. Good people, please be informed of this, please understand. *(sits at back corner)*

shidai music (The crowd and their leader come on stage to this entrance music and line up at the front of the stage. They are dressed in the matching vests and trousers of the average man and carry short swords.)

shidai CROWD & LEADER	*(facing each other at stage front)* Now at last the longed for time of cherry blossom quests, now at last the longed for time of cherry blossom quests, let us hurry to the spring scene of the hill paths.
nanori LEADER	*(turning to face front)* I that stand before you here am a man from southern Kyoto. Now when spring comes round I always go here and there and everywhere to see the cherry blossoms and spend my days in the fields and hills. Yesterday I went to have a look at Jishū Gongen's cherry tree in the Eastern Hills.[1] Today I hear that the blossoms at Saigyō's Hermitage in the Western Hills are in full bloom, so I am bringing a crowd of blossom viewers with me, and now we are hurrying on our way to Saigyō's Hermitage.
ageuta CROWD & LEADER	*(facing each other again)* "A hundred thousand trilling birds wake singing spring, trilling birds wake singing spring, to fresh life once more all around me is renewed."[2] I count the days now is the time the skies of early April. Ho there! my friends, friends of the flowers slow your step and stay a while to view the cherry blossom. Old friends and strangers gathered here are all at one and not a one but has a heart in flower, and not a one

[1] At Kiyomizu Temple.

[2] Most of the first four lines of *Kokinshū* poem 28 by an unknown poet. The last line of the original poem is "while I alone grow older."

but has a heart in flower.[3]
(leader steps to indicate travel)

tsukizerifu CROWD & LEADER	*(facing front)* We have travelled so fast. Here we are already at Saigyō's Hermitage.
LEADER	Everybody please wait here a while. I shall announce our arrival.
CROWD	Very well. *(go to the bridge)*
mondō LEADER	*(at first pine)* I beg your pardon. I wish to announce myself.
KYŌGEN	*(rising and going to the shite spot)* Who is it?
LEADER	I am a man from Kyoto. We heard that the cherry at this hermitage is in full bloom and have come all this long way to have a look at it. Won't you please let us see it?
KYŌGEN	It seems like a simple enough thing, but this year, flower viewing is forbidden here. However, since you have come such a long way, I'll find out what kind of humor my master is in and see if I dare tell him your request.
LEADER	Very well. *(to crowd)* Since that is how things are, wait here for a while all of you.

(All turn backs to stage and kneel. The kyōgen waits a while at the attendant spot.)

sashi WAKI	*(still sitting on stool at waki spot)* Ah, yes, indeed spring's blossoms blooming on the tall tree top show how the Bodhisattvas

[3]Echoes Chinese poems describing spring as the time when plants and hearts are in flower. The flower in figurative language means poetry.

rise to reach the Light
that is Truth's very heart.
The moon's reflection
in the pools of fall
show how the Bodhisattvas
plumb the depths
to bring that light
to all who lie in darkness.[4]
The flowing waters tell
when the hot summer days are done
and ah! how time runs on.
The winds that sweep the pines
far down the valley floor
with one voice warn us
of the fall that overtakes us
and thus all things that are
each in its way
teaches the Buddha's Law
and that is how the trees,
the grasses and the lands
will all reach Buddhahood.
Be that as may
of all four times of year
these two are best
the time of flowers
and the time of fruit.

mondō	*(kyōgen has gone to the shite spot)*
KYŌGEN	Why, there's not in all Japan a man in better humor. Let me say my say quickly.
	(goes to stage center and kneels)
	I beg your pardon, Sir. A crowd of people have come from the capital and say they would like to see the cherry blossoms in this garden.
WAKI	What? From the capital you say? Do you tell me these people have come out all the way here to this hermitage to see the cherry blossoms?
KYŌGEN	Yes, Sir, that is so.

[4]Variants of this passssage are also found in the Noh plays *Atsumori* and *Tōboku*.

WAKI   What? With all the city in bloom and every place in it famous
            for blossoms, while here at Saigyō's hill retreat there's noth-
            ing but one old, lone tree in flower! And then I am a hermit
            who has given up the world, but when the cherry tree draws
            people here, they find me out as well. I wonder if it is right,
            but since they have come all that way after their heart's de-
            sire, how can I send them home until they have seen it?
            Open the gate in the brushwood fence and have them come
            inside.
            (points his fan toward the shite spot)

KYŌGEN   Yes, I'll do that.

*(Kyōgen rises, goes to the shite spot and addresses the crowd who all rise and face
front.)*

mondō
KYŌGEN   Listen, you people. I have something to tell you. Since I
            broached the matter to my master when he was in rare good
            humor, he said to show you the flowers, so enter without de-
            lay.

CROWD   Yes, we understand.

*(Kyōgen goes to kyōgen spot and sits. Crowd and Leader come on stage chanting
and line up at stage right.)*

kakeai
CROWD &   "The cherry flowers
LEADER   must be out in glory now;
            in all the hollows
            of the foot-wearying hills
            are seen great white clouds massing"[5]
            and so we followed from afar
            and now we come to rest below this tree.
            (they sit at stage right)

WAKI   I come beneath the blossoms
            with another heart
            to contemplate
            the fall of flower and of leaf

---

[5]*Kokinshū* poem 59 by Ki no Tsurayuki.

and cleanse my hermit soul alone
and suddenly

CROWD &   high and low and rich and poor
LEADER   all manner of men have come
           and every one with a heart in full flower.

WAKI   I am as if returned to springs long gone.

CROWD   Although a hill retreat hid from the world,

WAKI   here now because of cherry flowers

CROWD   it is the flower capital.

ageuta
CHORUS   A monk may well renounce the world
           but how can flowers be hidden,
           but how can flowers be hidden?
           Because of them men find me.
           This place lies deep in Saga's craggy hills
           far from the haunts of men,
           but when the spring comes round
           the world of sorrows and the madding crowd
           still make their way to Saga.
           Ah yes, a man may want to flee the world
           but has no other place to live.
           Ah! Where shall I find my last home?
           Is there no place a man can be alone?
           (waki and crowd face each other)
           Is there no place a man can be alone?

mondō   *(to crowd)*
WAKI   Hear me, good people! You came all this long way spurred
           by most gentle feelings. However, for a hermit who has given
           up the world and had for sole companion this lone cherry
           tree, to find you flower-friends beneath it was not quite what
           he had in mind, so I was moved to make this poem:
           (turning to face front)
           "To see the flowers
           is the reason I am told
           why people flock here.

Hardly fitting, but the fault
lies with the wretched cherry tree."[6]

uta   *(waki gets off stool and sits on stage)*
CHORUS   And now below
that wretched cherry tree
fall shades of twilight;
dark is closing in,
but there's the moonrise
beneath the flowering tree
this moonlit night,
forgetting our way home
Oh! let us pass the night
and all night long look on the flowers
until the daybreak.[7]

(The crowd leave the stage through the little side door during the above passage. Then the cloth around the frame of the prop is lowered by the stage attendants revealing the shite, sitting on a stool. He has on an old man's mask with a white headband over long white hair on top of which is a stiff hat. He wears a hunting cloak over a brocade robe and red divided skirts.)

sashi   *(sitting inside the prop)*
SHITE   Like a buried tree
unknown to men
I too am hidden
but the flower still is in my heart[8]
"To see the flowers
is the reason I am told
Why people flock here.

[6]Saigyō's poem which appears both in his private anthology, the *Sankashū* and in the *Gyokuyōshū*, the 14th imperial anthology completed in 1313 or 1314.

[7]There are many echoes of T'ang Chinese poetry in this play, and the event of poet-friends spending a night under a flowering tree was a custom of Chinese poets and literati. Frequent mention of such nights is found in T'ang and later Chinese poetry. Also Japanese poem 72 of the *Kokinshū* is probably alluded to: *Kono sato ni/tabine shinubeshi/sakurabana/chiri no magai ni/ieji wasurete:* In this village here/I must sleep the traveller's sleep/Oh! Cherry blossoms!/The whirl of falling flowers/Makes me forget my way home. It means either that the poet was enjoying the cherry blossoms and slept with them under the tree or that he was enjoying drunken revels with prostitutes and slept it off at the inn.

[8]This can mean "I still have poetic talent."

Hardly fitting, but the fault
lies with the wretched cherry tree."

kakeai

WAKI   How strange a thing! From the rotted hollow of this old tree in flower now appears an ancient white-haired man reciting Saigyō's poem. What a strange being this is!

SHITE   I am an old man of dream, but I come before you now to question you about the meaning of the poem you have just made.

WAKI   Well, if you are an old man of dream you should come to me in my dreams. Be that as it may, why do you wish to question me about this poem I have just made? Are there any doubtful points in it?

SHITE   Oh no, how could there be doubtful points in a poem by the great priest Saigyō, but
"To see the flowers
is the reason I am told
why people flock here.
Hardly fitting, but the fault
lies with the wretched cherry tree."
Now what is the fault of the cherry tree?

WAKI   Oh! It is just that I who have cast off the sorrowful world to live as a hermit in this hill retreat, am nevertheless disturbed by people high and low who flock here. I find this a nuisance, so I wanted to express something of my feelings in a poem.

SHITE   If I may be so bold as to say so, such an attitude is open to question. The world of sorrows and the hill retreat are in a man's own heart, and the flowering of unfeeling trees and grasses has nothing to do with your human vale of tears. It is therefore without blame.

WAKI   What you say is reasonable, but is the one who reasons thus perhaps the spirit of some flowering tree?

SHITE   I am indeed the spirit of a flower, and I too have grown old under this cherry tree.

WAKI	"A flower is a plant that speaks no word,"[9]
SHITE	but I must show that I am blameless.
WAKI	"Reflected flowers open petal-lips,"
SHITE	so I part my lips now.

uta
CHORUS   *(looking down)*
Ah! But I am ashamed.
(stands, leaves prop, goes to center stage)
Flowers come few to an old tree
its limbs are weak and withered.
Ah! "the wretched cherry tree."
Wretched alas! in its forlorn state
but as for that fault
that you say lies with it.
Yes, lies indeed
it simply is not there;
I am the spirit of the flowering cherry.
(circles left to shite spot)
Even the trees and grasses
called unfeeling
(facing waki moves to center stage)
still never forget
(waki stands and moves toward shite)
their time of flowers
and their time of fruit.
Therefore in truth
(both kneel and pray)
the trees, the grasses and the lands
will all reach Buddhahood!

unnamed
SHITE   How blessed I am to have met the holy priest! I am blessed
with the dew of Buddha's Law. Ah! I recall

---

[9]There is a Zen dictum. 'A flower does not speak.' This is also a quote from Sugawara no Fumitoki's poem 117 in the *Wakan rōeishū*. The next waki line continues the quotation. This poem also occurs in *Unrin'in* and *Hōshigahaha*.

"Blossoms smile along the balustrade
though none can hear their flower voice;
birds are crying in the greenwood shade.
Oh! hard to stop their tears of joy."[10]

(As the shite goes to center back and stands facing front, the waki goes to sit at waki spot.)

kuri
CHORUS   "At morning treading fallen flowers
with a good friend I go out for a stroll;
at evening winging birds seek out their nests
along with them we make our way back home."[11]

sashi
SHITE   Although they flourish
in the fair nine-splendored city
the flowers bloom eight-fold.[12]

CHORUS   But oh! how many-fold
the springs piled over springs
that saw their flowering!

SHITE   Now, as for places famous for their flowers

CHORUS   first of all, the earliest to bloom,
my Lord Konoe's drooping cherry.[13]

kuse
CHORUS   *(shite dances a fairly standard kuse dance)*
"I look out over
willow fronds and cherry flowers
well interwoven,
the city rich arrayed

[10]A Chinese poem from the *Hyakuren shōkai*. The fourth line is modified from "tears of joy unceasing."

[11]Quotation from Po Chü-i, *Wakan rōeishū* poem 127.

[12]*Kokonoe no miyako*, the "nine-fold city," refers to its gates and its splendors. *Yaezakura*, "eight-fold cherry," is the name for a double cherry blossom.

[13]This is the first item in a catalogue of cherry blossoms. According to the *Gukanki* Konoe Michitsugu (1332-1387) had such beautiful weeping cherries that Shogun Yoshimitsu had some of them transplanted to his Muromachi palace in 1378.

in spring's brocade"[14]
her fitting raiment,
and here where once
a thousand trees were grown,
their peerless glory
gave its name to Senbon;[15]
in their flowering
we walk through cloudways
along roads deep under snow.
Bishamondō's blossoms, ah![16]
could even the flower glory
of the Four Kings' Realms
in Heaven above
excel their splendor?
(moving forward points up with fan)
Kurodani vale above
(lowers fan and looks down)
Shimogawara riverbed below
and Kachōzan the flower-topped hill

SHITE   where Bishop Henjō went to live
                 when long ago he fled the world.[17]

CHORUS   In the Eagle Hill's fast fading flowers
                 the sorrow-laden message
                 of the Craneswood stricken pale,[18]
                 at Kiyomizu Temple

---

[14]*Kokinshū* poem 56 by the priest Sosei. The last line is modified slightly.

[15]Senbon means "thousand trees." This refers to a major north-south street in Kyoto known as Senbon dōri, "thousand-tree street."

[16]A temple near the Eikandō in Kyoto's eastern hills. It no longer exists. Bishamon (alias Tamon) was one of the four great Heavenly Kings guarding the four directions.

[17]Kachōzan (Flower-Topped Hill) is one of the peaks of the Eastern Hills. There is confusion, surely deliberate, between it and Kazan or Hanayama near Uji in Yamashiro to whose temple the poet Yoshimine no Minesada retired after the death of Emperor Ninmyō (A.D. 850). He became the great poet-prelate Henjō Sōjō, one of the 36 Saints of Poetry.

[18]Refers to the blossoms of the Shōbōji (alias Eagle Hill) Temple, which in their fall proclaim the same message as the Sōrinji Temple in Kyoto's eastern hills that commemorates the death of Buddha. When he died everything in nature except the cat mourned him. Half of the twin-trunked Sala trees withered and the leaves, blighted by grief, turned ashen pale, the color of the crane's feathers. The message: everything must die, even Buddha.

Jishū Gongen's cherry flowers[19]
tell the self-same tale,
while on Otowa Hill of winged sounds
a tempest shakes the pines
and here again a stormtossed hill
Arashiyama[20]
whose innumerable blossoms
(waving pattern with fan)
with the water fall
cascading down Tonase rapids
in the Ōigawa
piling on the old stone dam
until it seems a weir of snow
holds back the rushing river.[21]
(ends dance at center back)

ei
SHITE   Already now, the rapid throbbing drum
sounds the last watch

CHORUS   and rings the late-night bell
(moves forward, performs open pattern)
resounding with it.

SHITE   Ah! sad to leave
the pleasures of this night!
Let us regret!
Let us regret!
Hard to come by
the right time,
hard to meet with
the true friend.
"A night in springtime

---

[19]Jishū gongen's tree at Kiyomizu Temple (also called Seisuji) is, now at least, a very unprepossessing tree, but it was a graft of a single cherry and a *yae*, the multipetalled variety. That makes it a nine-fold *kokonoe*, and its withering has a special message for *kokonoe no miyako*, the "nine-fold capital."

[20]There are plays on the place names. *Otowa* literally means "sound wings," while *arashi* means "storm."

[21]It was traditional in autumn poems to refer to the weir clogged with maple leaves from Arashiyama. A departure from the convention here.

a rare precious thing
of flower fragrance and of moonlight"[22]

waka   (*goes to shite spot to prepare for dance*)
SHITE   such a spring night was this one.

jonomai (The shite dances this slow, elegant dance to the music of the flute, the hand drums and the stick drum.)

waka   (*raising fan at shite spot*)
SHITE   This spring night,
from the flowers' shade
the dawn starts breaking

CHORUS   without waiting for the bell
it is time to part
it is time to part
it is time to part.

noriji
SHITE   Stay a while, oh stay a while
(*beckons waki with fan, moves to center*)
for still the night is deep.

CHORUS   (*shite looks at flower on stage prop*)
The brightness is the flowerglow.
Where there is no flower
(*circles right to shite spot*)
it is dark night still
in Mount Ogura's shadow
lying below the blossoms in the night
upon a flower pillow
(*wraps sleeve around arm to form pillow and kneels*)
we have dreamed a dream

uta   (*releases sleeve and looks up*)
SHITE   and now you wake from it,

CHORUS   (*shite stands and stamps*)
and now we wake from it.

---

[22]From a poem by the Sung poet Su T'ung Po.

The storm is over
in the stillness
scattered snow spread all around
"we tread the fallen flowers
(stamps again moving forward)
with hearts grown lonely
while we grieve too
for the gone spring of our youth."[23]
(circles left to shite spot)
The spring night broken into day,
the old man is gone
that old, old man
has faded soft away
(twirls sleeve, performs concluding stamps)
and left no trace.

---

[23]Alludes to a poem by Po Chü-i, number 27 in the *Wakan rōeishū*.

GENJI KUYŌ

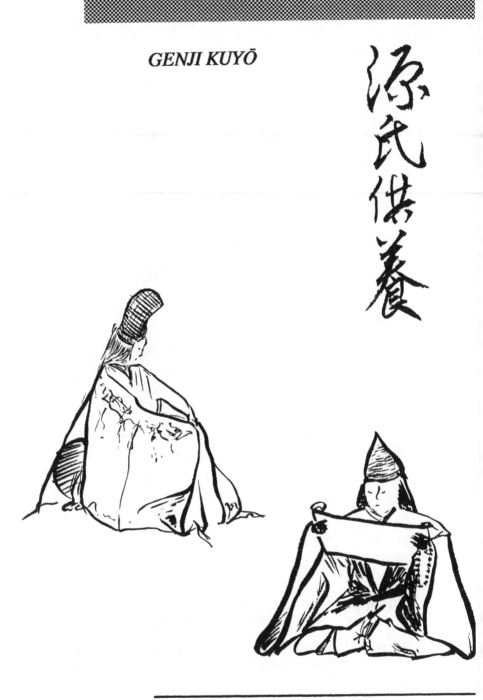

源氏供養

translated by Janet Goff

CHARACTERS

Waki: The incumbent priest of Agui Temple

Wakizure: Two priests

Shite
(act 1):   A woman of the place
(act 2):   The ghost of Murasaki Shikibu

SETTING: A spring day at the Ishiyama Temple near Lake Biwa where legend has it that Murasaki wrote the *Tale of Genji*.

AUTHOR: unknown

CATEGORY: A third-category, woman play. The stick drum is not used.

100

PERFORMANCE PRACTICES: Performed by all five schools. As the only dance to instrumental music in the standard version is a very brief *iroe*, several schools have variant performances which feature more dancing.

TEXT: The translation is based on the Kōetsu utaibon annotated in Itō 1986: 53-59. Several other texts were also consulted: Sanari 1930-31: 3, 1028-1040; Nogami 1971: 3, 113-124, Tanaka 1957: 1, 312-317,

SOURCES: *Genji monogatari*, a Kamakura period song called *Genji monogatari hyōbyaku*, and possibly a medieval tale known as *Genji kuyō sōshi*.

GENJI KUYŌ (A Memorial Service for Genji)

Translated by Janet Goff

ACT ONE

shidai music   *(The waki enters wearing a pointed hood, a dark travel robe, and white divided skirts. He carries a rosary. The wakizure who are similarly dressed follow him down the bridge to the stage.)*

shidai
WAKI &
WAKIZURE

(facing each other at stage front)
Wearing a humble robe
like moss along the road,
wearing a humble robe
like moss along the road,
to the temple at Ishiyama we go.[1]

nanori
WAKI

(facing front)
I am the incumbent priest of Agui Temple in Kyoto.[2] A devout follower of the Ishiyama Kannon, I often make pilgrimages there on foot.[3] I think I will do so again today.

ageuta
WAKI &
WAKIZURE

(facing each other)
Spring blossoms like
the capital from which I now set out,
the capital from which I now set out
in the rude wind,
white are the waves at dusk
on Shirakawa River; leaving it behind
I pass the waterfall at Otowa.
(waki takes a few steps to indicate travel)

---

[1]"Robe of moss" conventionally denotes a priest's robe because it suggests humble attire; "moss" anticipates "stone" in Ishiyama (Stone-Mountain). A branch of Shingon (esoteric) Buddhism, Ishiyama Temple is located a few miles east of Kyoto near Lake Biwa.

[2]Perhaps Chōken (1126-1203) or, more likely, his son Seikaku (1167-1235). Famous preachers and masters of *shōdō* (Buddhist prayers in Chinese set to music).

[3]The bodhisattva of mercy and compassion, Kannon enjoyed a great following in medieval Japan. Worship of the deity was closely associated with the *Lotus Sutra*.

102

Before the barrier lies the morning mist;
beyond it,
the lingering moon at dawn shines
on Biwa, the sea of grebes.[4]
What an interesting sight it is.
What an interesting sight it is.

sageuta   *(facing each other)*
By the gentle waves in Shiga,
on Kara Cape stands a solitary pine.
No salt is burned here,
yet the waves along the shore
send up a cloud of misty smoke,
send up a cloud of misty smoke.[5]
(they go to the waki spot)

mondō   *(calling out from behind the curtain)*
SHITE   If you please, I wish to speak to the incumbent priest of Agui
Temple.

WAKI   *(turning to face the shite)*
Are you addressing me?

*(The shite enters the bridge wearing a young woman's mask and a brocade ki-
mono.)*

SHITE   In seclusion at Ishiyama
I composed the sixty *Genji* chapters,[6]
an idle diversion that survived my death.
(stops at second pine)
My name is still remembered for it,
but I failed to hold
a memorial service for *Genji*,
and am thus condemned

---

[4]A poetic name for Lake Biwa; part of a catalogue of poetic place names *(uta makura)* which includes Shirakawa, Otowa Falls, and Kara Cape below.

[5]A common motif in court poetry, salt burning refers to the practice of boiling brine by the seashore with pine kindling to produce salt. The verb *tatsu* ("send up") suggests cresting waves, trees standing on the cape, and rising smoke.

[6]The *Genji* actually has fifty-four chapters, but was often referred to in the middle ages as having sixty, in imitation of the scriptures in Tendai Buddhism, which were collected in sixty volumes.

to wander without attaining salvation.
If possible, would you please at Ishiyama
hold a memorial service for *Genji*
and pray on behalf of my soul?
I have appeared here now
to ask this of you.

WAKI   Your request is easy to fulfill. I will gladly perform a memo-
                rial service, but for whom should I pray?

SHITE   *(coming on stage to the shite spot)*
                Just go to Ishiyama and hold a memorial service for *Genji*. I
                will appear there and pray together with you.

WAKI   I am delighted; it is an excellent idea.
                The person who wrote *Genji*...

SHITE   I am ashamed to say, has become part of the dust in this
                wretched world,

WAKI   but her name is not buried beneath the moss.[7]

SHITE   Over Ishiyama Temple lie clouds

WAKI   a lavender hue called *murasaki*.
                You must be the lady by that name.[8]

ageuta   *(looking down)*
SHITE   How ashamed I am.
                Is it apparent from the color?

CHORUS: Is it apparent from the color
                (looks up)
                of the clouds lit by the evening sun?
                (faces waki)

---

[7]"Name is not buried" *(na o ba uzumanu)* is a conventional poetic phrase. Izumi
Shikibu's poem in the *Kin'yōshū* (X, 612), "On the Death of Koshikibu," is a well-known
example: *morotomo ni/koke no shita ni wa/kuchizu shite/uzumarenu na o/kiku zo kanashiki*
(How sad I am/when I hear her name,/which has never/ died though she lies/buried beneath
the moss).

[8]Amida Buddha descends to earth on a cloud of lavender to welcome the souls of the
dead to the Western Paradise. Lavender *(murasaki)* also plays on the name Murasaki Shikibu.

Even now unable to state her name
(makes a small circle around the stage)
she vanished completely out of sight.
(exits down bridge)
She vanished completely out of sight.

INTERLUDE

(No interlude is currently performed; although there does appear to have been one in the early Tokugawa period.)

ACT TWO

WAKI   *(sitting in center stage)*
                We have made our way to Ishiyama,
                and our prayers have been completed.
                At this late hour, the sound of the bell
                and our hearts are clear.

WAKIZURE   That story we heard about *Genji*
                does not seem very convincing; still,

WAKI   let us perform a memorial service
                for Murasaki Shikibu's

WAKIZURE   salvation

WAKI   let us devoutly pray.

ageuta
WAKI &   Even so, in this fickle world,
WAKIZURE   even so, in this fickle world
                that fades into a dream, Murasaki emerged
                like a flower in a moment of glory
                only to disappear from sight,[9] and
                the tale of Radiant Genji long ago

[9]"Moment of glory" *(hana mo hitotoki)* alludes to *Kokinshū* poem 1016 by Bishop Henjō: *aki no no ni/namamekitateru/ominaeshi/ana kashigamashi/hana mo hitotoki*: In the autumn fields/the lovely lady-flowers/demurely bloom:/how bold they are/in their moment of glory.

somehow strikes me as a story
that cannot really be believed,
that cannot really be believed.[10]
(he goes to the waki spot and sits)

issei music *(The shite enters wearing a gauze cloak and red divided skirts. She has on a young woman's mask and a stiff black hat. A scroll is tucked into the breast of the kimono she wears under the cloak. She pauses at the first pine.)*

issei SHITE	*(facing forward)* Crimson leaves scattered on the mountainside: a telling memento of the wind in the pines. *(goes to shite spot)*
kakeai CHORUS	So, too, the name Murasaki is revealed.
SHITE	*(faces waki)* I am ashamed to be seen. *(looks down)*
WAKI	The night has deepened and the birds are still; at a forsaken hour the torch light reveals a beautiful woman lifting the hem of her lavender robe. Is the wraith-like figure standing there real or a dream?--I cannot tell.
SHITE	Beneath layered robes the color of flowers that swiftly fade is one, like hidden passion, deeply dyed. Even if the color cannot be seen, tracing my story to the end, like purple *hagi* in a withered field, should enable you to guess my name.[11]

---

[10]These words suggest doubt about the veracity of the *Tale of Genji* as well as the shite's words in act one.

[11]The shite's speech contains a rich mixture of puns and associated words connected with flowers, robes, and colors. *Kasane no kinu no shita kogare* has a play on *kogare[ru]*, which can mean "(underrobe) deeply dyed" as well as "yearn passionately for". Since the robe of deep lavender, which of course suggests Murasaki, lies under several other robes, it cannot be seen as

WAKI	Even if the color is not visible, you say-- I understand your point.[12] Are you Lady Murasaki, then?
SHITE	I am ashamed to say that this form,
WAKI	the figure I saw yesterday,
SHITE	remains the same today.
WAKI	Together, without reserve
SHITE	arising

uta
CHORUS	nor sleeping, let us stay awake 'til dawn.[13] *(shite looks up)* Take heed, oh moon, tonight along with the bell at Ishiyama Temple. *(shite makes small circle around stage)* Before the wind that chases dreams away a flame will die like the light long ago. *(stops at shite spot and turns toward waki)* Let us pray for Radiant Genji's soul, *(goes to center stage and sits)* let us pray for Radiant Genji's soul.[14]

kakeai
SHITE	I am grateful indeed. What sort of offering should I make?

readily as purple *hagi* (bush clover). Murasaki (lavender) and *moto no* ("root" or "source;" here, "story") are conventionally linked to *hagi* in *renga. (Renju gappeki shū,* no. 233 in Kido and Shigematsu 1972).

[12]*Kokoroenu* ("I understand") is taken by some commentators to be the negative form of the verb.

[13]Together the shite and chorus allude to a poem by Ariwara no Narihira in the *Kokinshū* (number 616) and in the *Tales of Ise,* episode 2. *Oki mo sezu/ne mo sede yoru o/akashite wa/ haru no mono tote/nagame kurashitsu:* Neither arising/nor sleeping, all night long/I stay awake,/ only to spend the days staring/at the endless rain of spring.

[14]The text suggests that Genji vanished from the world like the flame of a torch before the wind.

WAKI	I seek no offering. This world exists in a dream; recall the past with a wave of your sleeve and perform a dance here now.
SHITE	Though I am embarrassed, how can I ignore your request? Very well, I shall dance, she says and
WAKI	Murasaki, befitting her name,
SHITE	in a fine robe of lavender
WAKI .	with crimson cords, holds a fan the color of the setting sun
SHITE	*(standing)* as she shyly yet gracefully
WAKI	performs the dance
SHITE	of the butterfly.[15]
shidai CHORUS	*(shite faces front)* Dancing sleeves in a dream, dancing sleeves in a dream: oh to turn it into reality.
issei SHITE	*(goes to shite spot)* Layers of flower-tinted robes,
CHORU	Slovely sleeves of lavender.
iroe	*(the shite performs the brief "color dance")*
kuri SHITE	*(the shite goes to the front of the drummers)* Impermanence is revealed before one's eyes yet has no form.

[15]The name of a court dance and a *Genji* chapter title, "butterfly" (*kochō*) is used here because of its association with the story in the Chinese classic *Chuang-tzu* about a man who dreamt he was a butterfly and then wondered afterward whether he was a butterfly dreaming he was a man.

CHORUS   Life is like a dream;
what person lives a hundred years?
The althea's day of glory is the same.[16]

sashi
SHITE   It was here that lowly Murasaki Shikibu
sought divine assistance;
at Ishiyama Temple
invoking the vow of compassion,
she went into seclusion
and entrusted to her brush
the writing of this tale.

CHORUS   But, because she failed
to hold a memorial service,
the cloud of delusion has never cleared.

SHITE   *(turning to face waki)* This rare encounter

CHORUS   inspired a fervent prayer,
(takes out the scroll and hands it to waki)
which I have inscribed on a scroll
hoping to awaken from darkness.
(makes a prayer gesture)
May Radiant Genji's spirit
attain enlightenment.
(waki stands at stage left, opens scroll)

kuse   *(shite points to scroll with fan)*
CHORUS   Now, then,
Kiritsubo in the Paulownia Court[17]
vanished as swiftly as evening smoke
ascending to the Realm of Law above;
(waki puts scroll in his kimono and sits)
the leaves of words

[16]A familiar expression adapted from a couplet by Po Chü-i included in the *Wakan rōei-shū* (no. 291): In the end, pine trees wither after a thousand years;/the blossoms of the althea are granted a day of glory.

[17]In the kuse, a catalogue of chapter titles from the *Tale of Genji*, an effort has been made to follow Seidensticker's renderings wherever possible. *Kiritsubo* ("Paulownia Court") is the title of the first chapter and the name of Genji's mother, who died when he was very young. As in *Kakitsubata* this is a long, double kuse.

in the broom tree that night
(shite stands and dances to the following)
have turned into flowers strewn
from the Tree of Enlightenment.[18]
(shite stands and stamps foot)
Despise this world
empty as a cicada's shell
and understand that life
(shite makes a large circle)
is but dew on an evening face.
Welcomed by a cloud
the color of young lavender,
on the dais of
the flower picked at the end,
it matters not if colored leaves fall
during an autumn excursion.
Encountering by chance the Buddha's wisdom,
grasp the sacred tree
while praying for deliverance.[19]

SHITE   In the village of falling flowers[20]

CHORUS   it is impossible to escape the truth
                 that parting from loved ones causes pain.
                 There is but one path to take:
                 leave the waves of life and death
                 on Suma Bay and set out
                 to attain the Fourfold Wisdom,[21]
                 immersed like a channel buoy
                 (shite does a sweeping point)

[18]"Broom Tree" *(hahakigi)*, chapter 2, contains the famous "Rainy Night Judgment" scene in which young courtiers discuss the merits of women of different rank. "Tree of Enlightenment" refers to the bodhi tree under which the Buddha attained enlightenment.

[19]Chapters 3 ("Cicada's Shell"), 4 ("Evening Faces"), 5 ("Young Lavender") and 6 ("The flower picked at the end"--a literal translation of *suetsumuhana*, "The Safflower"). The text suggests the dais of the Lotus Blossom, on which believers hope to be reborn in the Western Paradise. Chapters 7 ("An Autumn Excursion") and 10 ("Sacred Tree").

[20]Chapter 11, which Seidensticker renders as "The Orange Blossoms."

[21]"Suma" is the title of chapter 12. "Fourfold Wisdom" translates *shichi enmyō* (perfect light of the four types of wisdom) possessed by the Buddha: the wisdom of the perfect mirror, equality, wondrous perception, and achieving metamorphosis.

in the light of Akashi Bay.[22]
(shite makes small circle)
Seek the path of salvation
while dwelling in the wormwood patch.
(faces front at shite spot)
The wind in the pines may blow
(holds fan at left shoulder, looks right)
but the rack of cloud from bad karma
will never be dispelled.
(goes forward, does feather fan, stamps)
In the endless winds of autumn,
clad in purple trousers and a cloak
of fine gold and forgiveness,[23]
aspire to the dais of the lotus flower
in heaven's highest sphere;
seek the true realm
(circles stage)
where the cypress pillar stands
(holds fan out, moves slowly down)
adorned with precious jewels.
Distracted by the fragrance
of a branch of plum, the human heart
is no steadier than dew on wisteria leaves,
a jeweled chaplet briefly worn,
(makes circle)
or the fleeting splendor
of a morning glory.[24]

[22]The title of chapter 14, *miotsukushi* ("Channel Buoys") also means "throwing oneself heedlessly into something," or "immersing oneself." *Akashi* (chapter 13) is homophonous with a word for "light".

[23]Chapters 15, 18, 19 and 30. "Fine gold and forgiveness" *(shima ninniku)* is a Buddhist term signifying that the Buddha, adorned with fine gold, meets all insult, anger, and the like, with forgiveness. *Genji hyōbyaku* has "mercy, compassion, and forgiveness" *(jihi ninniku)*; mercy and compassion are special attributes of the Bodhisattva Kannon.

[24]Chapters 31 ("Cypress Pillar"), 32 ("A Branch of Plum"), 33 ("Wisteria Leaves"), 22 ("Jeweled Chaplet"), and 20 ("Morning Glory"). "Jewel[ed]" *(tama)*, "dew" *(tsuyu)* and "radiance" *(hikari)* are associated words.

SHITE   *(in center of stage)*
                 Dwell by day in the shade
                 of the sandalwood tree of great renown,[25]

CHORUS   forgo high rank and office
                 and retire
                 to an eastern cottage.
                 Glory and pleasure
                 (does a low sweeping point pattern)
                 may be likened to a drifting boat,
                 man's life to a drake fly.
                 (makes a small circle)
                 Cross the floating bridge of dreams
                 and pray for the heavenly host to come.[26]
                 (raises fan, looks west)
                 Hail Amida Buddha of the West!
                 (holds fan high, makes a large circle)
                 From the sin of
                 wild words and fancy phrases
                 absolve Murasaki Shikibu
                 and grant her salvation
                 in the world to come.[27]
                 (points toward waki)
                 Together
                 (turns right, flaps hands together, stamps) they ring the bell,
                 (facing waki)
                 bringing the service to an end.

rongi   *(shite faces front at shite spot)*
CHORUS   How interesting indeed. In the dancer's
                 wake a cock cries out;
                 with a wave of the sleeve
                 dream returns to reality.

[25]"Dwell...tree" echoes the title of chapter 49, *yadorigi* ("Mistletoe", rendered by Seiden-sticker as "The Ivy"). In *na mo takaki tsukasa kurai* the word *takaki* means both "great (re-nown)" and "high (rank and office)."

[26]Chapters 50, ("Eastern Cottage"), 51, ("Drifting Boat," Seidensticker's "A Boat upon the Waters"), 52, ("Drakefly"), and 54, ("Floating Bridge of Dreams"), the last chapter of the *Genji*.

[27]"Wild words and fancy phrases" *(kyōgen kigo)* goes back to Po Chü-i's famous prayer accompanying the copy of his Collected Works he presented to a Buddhist library.

SHITE   For the soul of Radiant Genji
I have prayed; through the power of the Law
(faces waki)
I too may be reborn on the Lotus Flower.
Hope lies in the bond
with the flower feast.[28]

CHORUS   *(moves toward front of stage)*
Indeed, the radiance of an autumn morning

SHITE   by nightfall leaves no trace behind.

CHORUS   Dew on a morning glory,
(does sweeping point)
a flash of lightning:
what is not ephemeral
(shite steps back and looks down)
in this fickle world of misery?

kiri   *(shite waves fan left to right)*
After careful reflection, it seems clear,
after careful reflection, it seems clear
(looks up)
that the person known as Murasaki Shikibu
(goes to front of stage)
is the Ishiyama Kannon,
(circles stage)
who appeared briefly in this world
(faces waki)
to write the *Tale of Genji*.
(shite flips sleeve and does a double sweep with fan)
This, then, is a means to tell mankind
that the world is but a dream.
Precious is the vow revealed.
(goes to shite spot)
Even the floating bridge of dreams
are words expressed inside a dream,
(turns right, flips sleeve, stamps)
are words expressed inside a dream.

[28]Chapter 8 ("Flower Festival;" Seidensticker, "The Festival of the Cherry Blossoms"). *Hana no en* also means "bond with the [Lotus] flower," in other words, the flower festival is auspicious because it suggests the Lotus of the Western Paradise.

碇潛

IKARIKAZUKI

translated by J. Philip Gabriel

CHARACTERS

Waki: A travelling priest

Shite
(act 1):   An old fisherman
(act 2):   The ghost of Taira Tomomori

Tsure
(act 2):   Lady Niidono (grandmother)
Lady Dainagon no Suke (nurse)

Kyōgen: A villager

SETTING: Hayatomo Bay in Nagato Province, present- day Yamaguchi Prefecture. It is near Dannoura, the site of the Heike clan's final battle.

AUTHOR: Unknown. Probably written in the late Muromachi period.

CATEGORY: Classified as a second-category, warrior or a fifth-category, demon play.

PERFORMANCE PRACTICES: Performed by the Kanze and Kongō schools. When performed as a second category play the prop is not used and the two tsure do not appear in the second act.

TEXT: The text translated is from Sanari, 1930-31: 1, 247-262. The text and annotations in Nogami 1971 were also consulted.

SOURCES: The *Tale of the Heike*, Chapter 11.

117

IKARIKAZUKI (The Anchor Draping)

Translated by J. Philip Gabriel

ACT ONE

shidai music *(The waki enters, dressed in a pointed hood, a plain kimono under a travel cloak tied with a decorated waist band, and carrying rosary beads. In his robe is a copy of the sutras. He advances to the shite spot.)*

shidai WAKI	*(facing the back of the stage)* I will not wander with the clouds, I will not wander with the clouds; instead the moon will guide me to the West.
nanori WAKI	*(facing front)* I am a priest on my way from the capital. The Heike clan met their end at Nagato's shores, and as I am of the same lineage, I wish to pray for their repose. Thus I am now headed toward Nagato.
ageuta WAKI	As sad as the journey of life the one I set forth on today, the one I set forth on today. I, a man of no fixed abode, having turned my back on the world to wander without destination, have arrived at Hayatomo Bay, where breakers seethe and *(takes a few steps to indicate journey)* tide and wind are strong.[1]
WAKI	*(facing front)*

---

[1]*Shio kaze haya/tomo no ura: haya* pivots to mean "(the salt wind blows) quickly (fiercely)" and to form part of the name Hayatomo Bay, the area of the sea off the straits of Shimonoseki in Nagato. Dannoura is the area directly to the north of it. Hayatomo Bay is described in the *Tale of the Heike* as a place of "seething tides."

WAKI	*(facing front)*
	My hurried steps have brought me to Hayatomo Bay.
	I will wait here for a boat to pass and try to take passage.
	(goes to waki spot and kneels)

issei music *(The shite enters wearing a "smiling old man" mask and an old man's wig. He is dressed in a plain kimono under a travel cloak, a straw apron with sash, and has a fan. Holding a pole, he advances to the shite spot.)*

issei

SHITE	As the shore plovers
	call out to their fellows,
	so too we fishing folk.
	Take heart![2]
	(the waki stands and faces the shite)

[mondō]

WAKI	Say there! I would like passage on your boat.
SHITE	Certainly. Have you the fare?
WAKI	One such as myself who has retired from this life does not have money for fares.
SHITE	How impudent you priests are! Do you think you can take passage without paying, especially over this frightful place, between Moji and Akama, where sea and wind are rough?[3]

---

[2]In a 1696 version of the play (cited in Sanari 1930-31: 1, 262) the shite had the following lines, which appeared before the mention of the shore plovers: *ika ni ami no mura kimi/kefu wa asanagi no sono mama ni/oki mo isobe mo nami wa nashi/ tsurutaruru itoma mo oshi ya toku ide/ukiyo no waza o iso to yo* (Well now, fisherfolk of the village. Today the morning calm is unbroken, and the sea and shore know no waves. With regret over even a moment away from fishing, let us hurry to do the work of this sad world.)

[3]Moji is in northern Bizen (present-day Fukuoka Prefecture); Akama is present-day Shimonoseki in Yamaguchi Prefecture. Between them lies the Hayatomo Strait separating Honshu and Kyushu.

WAKI   What a strange thing you say! It is the person who requests fare from a priest with no ties to this world, who is the impudent one.

SHITE   Well, that makes some sense. Now what is that thing hanging around your neck?[4]

WAKI   This is the *Lotus Sutra*. If you wish, I could recite it for you.

SHITE   I would be pleased if you would. A recitation of the sutra could then serve as your fare.

WAKI   As I board this boat, the boat of Buddhist Law,

SHITE   let us hear the recitation of the *Lotus Sutra*. So the words will be clearer, let us make brighter the torches.[5]

(The two of them kneel, the waki at the waki spot, the shite at center stage. The waki takes his copy of the sutra from his robe and opens it.)

WAKI   The *Lotus Sutra*, chapter 22,
            on the Yaku Bodhisattva:
            "As a child finds its mother,
            we find a boat
            for the crossing."[6]

---

[4]In current stage practice the copy of the sutra is usually tucked in the waki's robe. The fisherman's words may be interpreted as showing he is still interested in the fare and suspects the priest may have money on his person.

[5]*Iza chōmon sen hokekyō no moji no seki no to akaseya kagaribi*: the meaning of *moji* pivots from the "letters" (i.e. words) of the sutra to the place name; and *akaseya* means both to "open" (the barrier gate at Moji) and "make brighter" (the torches).

[6]The chapter relates how the Yaku Ō Bodhisattva (the Bodhisattva Medicine King) burned his body as an offering to Buddha. The passage quoted is from the following section of the sutra (translated by Hurvitz, 1976: 299): "As a chilled person finds fire, as a naked person finds clothing, as a merchant finds a chief, as a child finds its mother, as a passenger finds a ship, as darkness finds a torch, as a poor person finds a jewel, as the people find a king, as a commercial traveler finds the sea, as a candle dispels darkness, this scripture of the Dharma Blossom also, in the same way, can enable the beings to separate themselves from all woes, from all sickness and pain."

SHITE   Exactly.   So you have found your "boat for the crossing."   A most precious teaching indeed.

(The waki puts away his sutra, and the shite stands.)

ageuta
CHORUS   Quickly, get on board.

(The waki goes in front of the shite, in the middle stage front, and kneels as though boarding a boat.)

CHORUS   Quickly, get on board.
                 Our prayers are answered
                 on this boat of prayers.
                 Prayers of a priest
                 do make a fine fare.
                 On the boat pledged to take
                 us all across, the Law rides with us.
                 How thankful we are for the
                 ties that bind us even now,
                 ties that bind us even now.[7]

mondō
SHITE   We have arrived.   You may get off.

WAKI   *(going toward the waki spot)*
                 Old man. Please get off the boat, too.
                 I have something to ask of you.

SHITE   With pleasure.

(Shite throws down his pole, goes to center stage, and kneels.   Waki kneels at waki spot.)

WAKI   It is unbecoming for a priest to make such inquiries, but I would like to hear the tales of the battles fought here in days long gone.

SHITE   A simple matter it is you ask.
                 Let me relate the tale.

---

[7]The pledge refers to Buddha's pledge to leave not a single soul behind on the crossing to paradise. The boat here is likened to this pledge.

katari	*(shite sits on a stool and takes out fan)*
SHITE	In the battle of Dannoura
	the Heike knew they had lost.
	Noritsune, the second son of Norimori,[8]
	boarded a small ship,
	and thrusting forward with his halberd
	slashed out here and there,
	killing many enemy troops.
	About this time, Tomomori[9]
	sent a messenger to him:
	"Your behavior is unbecoming, Noritsune.
	If only you could find
	a more worthy opponent."
	Noritsune understood this to mean
	he should engage the enemy's general,
	and pressed on among the Heike boats
	in search of Yoshitsune.
kakeai	
CHORUS	Somehow he landed aboard
	the very boat Yoshitsune[10] was in.
SHITE	Happy at his good fortune,
	Noritsune began to slash away.
CHORUS	Seeing this, Yoshitsune
	Seeing this, Yoshitsune
	realized he was outclassed,
	and clutched his halberd
	to his side and leaped lightly
	to an ally's boat
	some twenty feet away.
	There was nothing Noritsune could do.
	He threw down his halberd
	and stood there angrily,

[8]Taira no Noritsune (1160-1185) was the son of Norimori and the nephew of the Heike leader Kiyomori. He is depicted in the *Tale of the Heike* as a leading Heike warrior.

[9]Taira no Tomomori (1152-1185), another leader of the Heike, was the son of Kiyomori and Niidono. He also appears in the noh play *Funa Benkei*.

[10]Minamoto Yoshitsune (1159-1189), half-brother of Yoritomo, the leader of the Genji, was the commander in charge of Minamoto forces at Dannoura. As evident in the play *Yoshino Shizuka*, he is later hounded by Yoritomo.

roaring at the enemy
and glaring at the scene around him.

SHITE   At that very moment,

CHORUS   at that very moment
a Genji warrior named Tarō
from Aki Province in Tosa,
and his brother Jirō,
pushed forward in their boats
and attacked Noritsune.[11]

SHITE   "To deal with such prideful men
(tucks his fan in his sash)

CHORUS   neither long nor short sword
do I need.
Now then--won't you come with me
to the land beyond the living?"
So saying he thrust out his arms,
(extends both arms)
grabbed the two men
and pulled them towards him.
With one man under each arm
he leaped into the waves
and sank.
(slips off stool and sits on stage)
SHITE   In truth we are[12]
(stands)

CHORUS   the ghosts of those
who sank into the waves.
Please pray for our repose,
please pray for our souls.
(exits quietly down bridge)

[11]The Genji warriors referred to are the sons of Saneyasu, head of Aki District in Tosa Province. Taro (Aki Tarō Sanemitsu) is described in the *Tale of the Heike* as having the strength of thirty men.

[12]The use of the plural (*hitobito*) here seems to refer to Tomomori and Lady Niidono who appear in act two, as well as Noritsune himself.

INTERLUDE

(At the waki's request, the kyōgen, a local villager, relates some of the background of the battles leading up to the Heike's final defeat, and goes on to tell the story of the death of Noritsune which was related in act one and of the deaths of Lady Niidono[13] and the young Emperor[14] portrayed in act two. The waki relates how the old fisherman in act one had told him the story of Noritsune's final battle and then disappeared. The kyōgen urges the waki to remain a while to pray for the souls of the Heike.)

ACT TWO

(The stage attendants bring out a roofed boat prop surrounded by a curtain and place it in front of the musicians.)

uta
WAKI   In the deep stillness of the night
        I sit by the seaside and pray for
        the Heike clan's repose.
        (looks towards the boat)
        How odd!
        Where there was nothing
        a large boat has appeared,
        and in the swift seas of Hayatomo
        it floats,
        carried by neither current
        nor oars.
        This is not the shore of
        Hsunyang Inlet,
        yet a wondrous melody
        is heard from the boat.[15]

[13]Taira no Shishi (Tokiko), the principle wife of Kiyomori and mother of both Tomomori and Kenreimon'in, the mother of the Antoku Emperor. Niidono is called Nun of the Second Rank in McCullough's translation of the *Tale of the Heike*.

[14]The Antoku Emperor (1178-1185), son of Kenreimon'in, Kiyomori's daughter, ascended the throne when he was two and died at 6 or 7 by Western count.

[15]An allusion to the poem "Song of the Lute," by the T'ang poet Po Chü-i written in 816. Assigned to a post in Hsunyang on the Yangtze, far from the capital, Po heard the sound of a lute being played on the river one night. "Listening to its tone," he wrote in a preface to the

The wafting koto strains ring clear,
unmuffled by pine breezes
or waves crashing on the cliffs.
Truly a thing most odd.

sashi
NIIDONO
(from inside the covered boat)
Lady Dainagon,[16]
tonight the waves are still,
so let us enjoy viewing the moon.
Please have the rush blinds removed.

(As the chorus sings, the stage attendants remove the covering from around the boat. Inside are revealed the ghosts of Taira Tomomori, Lady Niidono, and Lady Dainagon. Tomomori wears a warrior spirit's mask, a black wig and white headband. He has on a hat with two spade-shaped horns representing a war helmet. He wears a man's brocade kimono and broad, divided skirts under a three-quarter length cloak. Lady Niidono wears the mask of an aged woman, and a nun's hood. Over her satin-like under kimono she wears a brocade kimono with small sleeves. Lady Dainagon has on a young woman's mask and a wig with a hairband around it. Her costume is similar to Lady Niidono's except that it includes red which signifies her youth.)

ageuta
CHORUS
With but an oar for a pillow
at least we can await
the moon and the wind,
at least we can await
the moon and the wind
may sough through the pines.
Do remove the blinds.
In our night boat,
let us await the moon.

kuri
CHORUS
Examining fate, one compares it
to the plants on the shore.

poem, "I could detect a note of the capital in its clear twanging....I realized for the first time just what it meant to be an exile" (Translation by Watson, 1984: 249).

[16]Dainagon no Suke, one of the Antoku Emperor's nurses and a lady-in-waiting to Kenreimon'in, was the wife of Taira Shigehira, brother to both Kenreimon'in and Tomomori.

Human life is like a boat
cut adrift from its mooring.[17]

sashi
NIIDONO   At the battle of Dannoura
               when all hope was lost

CHORUS   the New Middle Councillor Tomomori
               turned to Lady Niidono
               and said,
               "The end is upon us.
               However painful it may be,
               you must accompany the Emperor
               beneath the waves.
               To a man we will join you."[18]

kuse
CHORUS   Holding back tears he spoke,
               and Lady Niidono listened to his words.
               "I understand," she said
               and calmly arose.
               Aware that this was her final attire,
               she tucked up the hem
               of her white skirts.
               The sacred jewel
               she clutched to her side,
               the sacred sword
               she placed in her sash,
               and to Lady Dainagon
               she entrusted the sacred mirror.[19]
               Kneeling before the royal throne she spoke.
               "May it please your majesty.
               Our land abounds

[17]An allusion to *Wakan rōeishū*, poem 790 on the topic of impermanence by Gen I (dates unknown) of the T'ang Dynasty. The plants referred to are rootless sea grasses, which, like the untethered boat, float unattached to the shore.

[18]Tomomori is somewhat cruder in the *Tale of the Heike*, where it is Niidono who makes the decision to jump overboard with the emperor (McCullough 1988: 178-79).

[19]The jewel, sword, and mirror are the Three Treasures (*sanshu no jingi*), symbols of imperial authority. Quite soon after the suicide of Niidono, Lady Dainagon no Suke attempted to follow her mother-in-law into the waves, but was foiled in her attempt by the Genji, who recovered the sacred mirror (McCullough 1988: 378-9).

with traitors and rebels.
Beneath those waves
lies a place called the Dragon Palace,
a most wonderful capital.
Let us make a journey there."
Tear after tear
trickled down her face
as she spoke.

NIIDONO   As might be imagined,
                the Emperor was frightened.

CHORUS   Tears streamed down his face
                as he faced east
                to bid farewell to the
                Goddess Amaterasu.
                Next he turned west,
                and had not yet
                said his prayers ten times
                when Lady Niidono approached.
                Holding him tightly,
                she closed her eyes and
                plunged into the waves.
                What use is it to speak of these
                bitter happenings now?
                Pray for our souls' repose,
                she beseeches the priests time and again
                the whole night long.[20]
                Suddenly the sky clouds over
                (the shite and two tsure stand)
                and a war cry pierces the air.

hayafue music   (*The tsure, Lady Niidono and Lady Dainagon, exit
by the side door.   The shite, the ghost of Tomomori, holding a halberd, goes to center stage.*)

noriji
SHITE   The *asura* battle

---

[20]The plural in the text (*sōtachi*) implies that the waki has other priests accompanying
him. They do not appear on stage.

CHORUS   is about to begin.[21]

kakeri (To instrumental music the shite performs a brief dance which reflects the agonies of battle through its irregular rhythms.)

SHITE   Who are these beings
            floating up on the waves?
            Is that the *asura* general
            known as the king of ignorance?[22]
            Look! Great numbers of armed guards,
            imperial advisers
            of the third rank,
            the sovereign's
            private councillor.[23]
            All the former Heike ranks
            with shields thrust out,
            rout your foes!
            How bitter that our *asura* wrath
            bursts forth once again.

chūnoriji
CHORUS   The *asura* battle has begun.
            (shite stamps)
            The *asura* battle has begun.
            (goes to corner)
            Genji troops in great numbers float up
            (circles left)
            and surround the royal boat.
            (goes to front stage)
            How fiercely the battle is met.[24]

[21]The asura realm, one of the six courses of transmigration (*rokudō*), represents a state of constant fighting.

[22]*Mumyō* is a Buddhist term defined as "darkness (of mind)," or "ignorance." A related term is *mumyō no umi* which could be translated as "the sea of ignorance" or "the realm of spiritual darkness" (Inagaki, 1984: 214).

[23]For the sake of keeping some of the conciseness of the original text, the translation simplifies what is a slightly more detailed list of Heike warriors and officials. The armed guards are of two different ranks, while the private councillor (secretary is another translation) referred to is listed as serving concurrently as a controller of the Great Council of State.

[24]Alternate lines are: *Gozabune ni wa me mo kakezu. Tada heisen ni zo kakarikeru:* "Ignoring the royal boat, they attacked the troop ships" (Sanari 1930-31: 1, 261).

SHITE   The Heike courtiers rush to
         (lunges forward with halberd)
         stern and bow.

CHORUS   The Heike courtiers stand at
         (goes to back stage left)
         stern and bow,
         their arrows at the ready.
         Sword tips in array,
         they await the enemy's approach.
         (stares at corner)
         From among them
         Tomomori stands forth.
         His halberd thrust out far
         (mimes fighting with halberd)
         he slashes out to the left
         and scatters enemies to the right,
         slaying many of the Genji clan.
         (jumps and falls to knees)
         'This is the end.
         I'll drown myself,' he thinks,
         (stands and goes toward attendants)
         and dons two suits of armor
         (substitutes fan for halberd, goes to center stage)
         and two helmets.
         To make himself more heavy still,
         from far off the shore
         he hauls up a great anchor rope,
         (mimes the pulling up of anchor)
         straining at the task.
         On top of his helmets
         he drapes the anchor,
         (puts both hands on head)
         he drapes the anchor.[25]
         (falls to knees)
         And leaps into the water,
         sinking to the sea's very floor.
         (goes to shite spot and stamps)

___

[25]It is interesting to note that despite the title of the play, the expression here translated as "drapes an anchor" is not *ikari o kazuku,* but *(kabuto no ue ni) ikari o itadaki*: "wearing an anchor on top of his helmet." In the *Tale of the Heike* it is not Tomomori, but Norimori (Noritsune's father) who use anchors to weigh himself and his brother down. The phrase used there is *yoroi no ue ni ikari o oi*: "on top of their armor they hung anchors."

YOSHINO SHIZUKA

translated by *Etsuko Terasaki*

CHARACTERS

Waki: Satō Tadanobu

Shite: Lady Shizuka

Omo Kyōgen: A monk-soldier in Yoshino

Ado Kyōgen: Another monk-soldier

SETTING: A spring day on Yoshino Mountain, Yamato Province. Early Kamakura period, sometime before Yoshitsune's death in 1189.

AUTHOR: Attributed to Kan'ami (Kanze Kiyotsugu), possibly revised by Iami.

CATEGORY: This play is classified either as a third-category, woman play or as a fourth-category, contemporary play.

PERFORMANCES PRACTICES: All five schools currently perform this play; however, only Konparu and, until quite recently, Kita perform both acts. The other schools perform only the second act.

TEXT: The translation is based on Yokomichi and Omote 1960-63: 1, 89-95.

SOURCES: The *Tale of the Heike*, chapter 11, and the *Gikeiki*, chapter 5.

TRANSLATIONS: Tyler 1978: 91-99.

YOSHINO SHIZUKA (Lady Shizuka in Yoshino)

Translated by Etsuko Terasaki

ACT ONE

(The shite, Lady Shizuka, walks quietly down the bridge to the stage. She is wearing a brocade kimono without a divided skirt. She sits at the waki spot.)

shidai music *(The waki enters the stage and stops at the shite spot. He wears a short, sleeveless coat with black court cap. A bow is in his left hand and an arrow in his right.)*

shidai	*(stands at shite spot, facing the back.)*
WAKI	In this uncertain world
	in this topsy-turvy world,
	my wretched fate indeed may turn
	into good fortune.

nanori	*(facing front)*
WAKI	I am Satō Tadanobu,[1] a retainer of Lord Lieutenant Yoshitsune.[2] Since he and his older brother, Yoritomo, are now in discord, my lord took refuge in this mountain, thinking it was safe.[3] But because the monk-soldiers here have changed their allegiance, he is going to retreat tonight. I have received his order to stay and hold off the enemy with my ar-

---

[1]SatōTadanobu (1161-1186), a son of Satō Shōji (d. 1189). Together with his brother Tsuginobu (1158-1185), he served Yoshitsune and stayed behind in Mt. Yoshino to fend off the enemies and let his master escape. He later committed suicide in Kyoto.

[2]Minamoto no Yoshitsune (1159-1189). The title *hogan* denotes his court rank of *kembiishi* (police commissioner); it eventually became his popular appellation. Yoritomo is Yoshitsune's older brother, who established a new feudal headquarters at Kamakura, away from the capital and the influence of the court, in order to consolidate power wholly in his own hands. With the once-powerful Heike clan out of the way, he did not hesitate to eliminate rival members of his own family in the most deliberate and ruthless way. Consumed with envy of Yoshitsune's military success, Yoritomo sent assassins to kill him and a long manhunt ensued.

[3]Mt. Yoshino in central Nara Prefecture. It was a major base for the training of yamabushi, the mountain ascetics, and also a stronghold of the monk-soldiers stationed at the Konrin Temple, where the tutelary deity, Zaō Gongen, was worshipped.

ceived his order to stay and hold off the enemy with
my arrows. Considering that it is the highest honor
for a samurai, I alone have stayed behind in this
mountain.   I understand that there will be a meeting
of the monk-soldiers at the Great Lecture Hall.   I
shall mix with the pilgrims from the capital, enter
the Lecture Hall, and listen to their deliberations.

sashi   *(still facing front)*
WAKI   Though we take example
             from the past,
             our wretched fortune will not change
             In days of old, Kiyomihara,[4]
             who later was to become emperor,
             was attacked by Prince Otomo.
             He was expelled from Yoshino Palace
             and roamed the fields, I hear.
             How pitiful!
             My Lord Lieutenant, too,
             since he has not been cleared
             of slanderous accusations,[5]
             must hide in clouds
             deep in Yoshino mountain.
             But at this hiding place too
             he can remain no longer.
             How sad is his future!
             To what hamlet will my lord
             escape? It concerns me deeply.
             Fearfully, I look at
             the distant sky of beautiful[6]

ageuta
WAKI   Yoshino mountain!
             The waterfall among the flowers,

---

[4]Kiyomihara refers to the place where Emperor Tenmu (the 40th), a younger brother of
Emperor Tenchi, was enthroned. As Prince Oama, he contested the imperial rule with Prince
Otomo (the son of Emperor Kōbun), resulting in the Jinshin Rebellion of 672. He was able to
retain his stronghold in Mt. Yoshino, and later his forces won him the throne.

[5]Yoshitsune was slandered on many occasions by one of Yoritomo's high-ranking retainers, Kajiwara no Kagetoki, who was extremely jealous of Yoshitsune.

[6]*Sora o mi yoshino: mi* pivots to mean "see (the sky)" and "beautiful (Yoshino)" in a typi-
cally economical Noh manner.

floating like mist,
the waterfall among the flowers,
floating like mist,
where does it go?
No one knows the fate
of the white ripples.
On whom shall I depend[7]
in deep Yoshino?
My future is wretched!
Although my lord and I
are separated
our hearts are one.
We must take two different paths
although it is only for a short time![8]
How confusing,
this aimless roaming!

mondō   *(turning to face shite)*
              Well, isn't this Lady Shizuka?[9]

SHITE   *(remains seated)*
              Is that you, Tadanobu?

WAKI   *(goes to center stage and sits)*
              Yes, madam. Because I was ordered to stop the pur-
              suers, I alone stayed behind. My lord made his es-
              cape. What will you do now, Lady Shizuka? I am
              truly sorry for your fate.

SHITE   Indeed! I believed
              that even though my lord
              took refuge in Yoshino,
              distant as far away China,
              I should

---

[7]A play of homonyms between *yoshi* of Yoshino and *yoshi*, "to rely on."

[8]Related words containing numbers: "hearts are *one*," "take *two* different paths," and "*four* a short time" (*shibashi*).

[9]A favorite mistress of Yoshitsune, who was pregnant at the time. Later she was captured and brought before Yoritomo. Famous as a shirabyōshi dancer, she was forced to perform before her enemy. In the end she retreated to a temple as a nun. The shirabyōshi was a type of courtesan-entertainer, who came into existence toward the end of Heian period. They danced and sang the popular ballads of the time in man's attire.

never be left behind.[10]
But I see now how worthless
I am, as a woman!
I was abandoned in Yoshino,
lost in the mountains,
hiding in the hamlets,
here I am in this hapless situation.

WAKI

(looks toward stage right)
Oh, I hear the sounds of the temple bell and the
blaring of the conch shell near the Great Lecture
Hall.
(faces front)
I can guess what that sound means.   Those must be
the conch and bell signals for the meeting of the
monk-soldiers to discuss the pursuit of our lord. A
good plan just came to me.
(faces shite)
Why don't you, my lady, go to the Katte shrine[11]
and offer a sacred dance to the deity.   I shall pretend to be a pilgrim from the capital and also go to
the shrine.   The monk-soldiers will surely ask me
about the capital.   I shall tell them that the brothers,
Lords Yoritomo and Yoshitsune, have finally made
up. In this way, I shall try to cause a delay so as to
let our lord escape further in peace.
As Tadanobu thus makes his plan,
he realizes he has only himself
to rely upon. What if his plot
is discovered?

SHITE

Our anxieties sink us deeply in
tears in Yoshino.   Even if
we are captured, our main purpose
will be achieved only if
our lord is able to escape.
That is all that matters.

---

[10]A rephrasing of lines from *Kokinshū* poem 1049 by Fujiwara Tokihira.

[11]Katte Myōjin. Together with Kimori Myōjin, the two make up the twin manifestations
of Zaō Gongen, the tutelary deity of Yoshino mountain.

(The waki rises and goes to the stage attendant spot where he sits down.   The shite rises.)

ageuta
CHORUS   Tadanobu, so resolved,
              Tadanobu, so resolved
              enters the Great Lecture Hall
              to attend the monk-soldiers' discussion.

SHITE   Shizuka presents herself
              (goes to shite spot)

CHORUS   before the deity Katte,
              Shizuka presents herself
              before the deity Katte.
              (exits down bridge)

(With the help of the stage attendants the waki takes off his head-gear and swords, and puts on a robe and a straw hat.)

INTERLUDE

(The omo kyōgen appears on the bridge wearing an sleeveless vest over a plaid kimono and trousers tied at the ankles. The ado kyōgen, similarly dressed, follows omo down the bridge. They imitate the blowing of conch shells.)

OMO   *Tsu-wai, tsu-wai.*

ADO   *Tsu-wai, tsu-wai.*

(They enter the stage and circle it repeating the sounds.)

mondō   *(facing ado)*
OMO   Why in the world are the others late in coming?

ADO   Yes, it is strange they are late.

OMO   Let's sit here and wait.

(They sit right and left of center front. Tadanobu stands up at the attendant spot and goes and sits between the two soldiers, a little behind them.)

OMO   Hey you! What on earth are you doing, sitting here at the meeting place of the monk-soldiers, from all the eighteen hamlets of Yoshino? Get up!
(angrily, the soldier questions Tadanobu)

WAKI   I am a pilgrim from the capital. I did not realize this was a meeting place for the monk-soldiers. Will you forgive me?

OMO   If he is a pilgrim from the capital, I'll ask him; he must know.

ADO   Good, ask him!

(The monk-soldier asks Tadanobu about Yoshitsune.)

WAKI   Lords Yoritomo and Yoshitsune are blood brothers. Let me report to you that they have finally been reconciled.

OMO   How many soldiers did the Lord Lieutenant have with him when he retreated? Do you know?

WAKI   I hear there were twelve horsemen.[12]

OMO   Oh, that is not many. Our strength, yours and mine, will be enough. Let us go after them!
(The two soldiers impulsively stand up.)

WAKI   Wait a moment!
I said twelve, but they are as strong as a
large cavalry detachment
of one hundred, two hundred!
I am from the capital.
I am telling you this because I believe
in the Buddha of this mountain.
I only pray that this temple

---

[12]The *Gikeiki* lists sixteen retainers.

as well as the pilgrims' cells
may be safe from the warfare.
Oh, well, anyway...

ageuta
CHORUS   Do as you please in Yoshino mountain,
                do as you will, in Yoshino mountain.
                This is idle talk.
                If this leaks out to the Lord Lieutenant,
                he will blame me.
                I shall leave now.
                I shall take my leave.

(Waki rises and seats himself in back corner.)

OMO   Well, in that case,
                we also shall take our leave.
                Get away, get away!

*(Both soldiers quickly exit through the curtain. Waki goes to sit at
the waki spot.)*

ACT TWO

ashirai music   *(The shite, dressed in a white unlined kimono with
black headgear, quietly enters the stage, and stands at the shite spot
or by the first pine facing front.)*

SHITE   Well, here am I, Shizuka,
                wearing my formal dance costume,
                I await Tadanobu, who is late.
                I have kept my promise to him.

mondō   *(faces shite from the waki spot)*
WAKI   I am a pilgrim from the capital.
                Having heard that Lady Shizuka
                will perform the sacred dance,
                I decided to delay my return trip.
                Will you begin your dance a little early?

SHITE   *(at shite spot)*
                Oh, are you from the capital?
                How I long for it.

What are the tidings about the Lord Lieutenant's
narrow path of life?
A person from the capital must know something
about it.

WAKI   Since they have heard that the brothers made peace,
the people in the capital regret very much their former indiscretion in expelling Yoshitsune.   Everyone
is afraid.

SHITE   How happy I am. You, sir, from the capital, know
so much about my lord.

WAKI   I have talked too much!
Much time is lost.
Don't let your dance betray you.

SHITE   Yes, indeed!
Those who talk too much lack dignity.
We have been trying to give
a show of truth.
People may suspect us of being allies.
Let us not ever give ourselves away.[13]

issei   *(facing front)*
SHITE   Play the music gracefully
for the sacred dance of Shizuka![14]

CHORUS   The monk-soldiers are forgetting
their fierce intent to pursue Yoshitsune.

SHITE   The gods, too, must gladly accept
this dance offering of mine.

CHORUS   Indeed, Shizuka's dance is an offering
for a peaceful reign.[15]

---

[13]*Katte*, "ever" and the deity Katte are homonymous.

[14]Shizuka also means graceful, quiet, peaceful, etc., here to emphasize her action.

[15]*Miyo mo shizuka ga mai: shizuka* means both "peaceful (reign)" and "Shizuka's (dance)."

iroe (The shite dances a brief, graceful dance, circling the stage once to instrumental music.)

kuri
CHORUS   Our god's power and dignity
            increase by the people's worship
            and the believers benefit
            from his protection.[16]

sashi   *(at center back)*
SHITE   The Lord Lieutenant sincerely followed
            the way of the gods
            and respected the Imperial House.

CHORUS   He excelled in his loyal duties,
            never worked for his own private gain.

SHITE   Despite this he was slandered.

CHORUS   It is said
            "The gods dwell in an honest head.[17]

SHITE   I pray you, god Katte, to stay
            on Shizuka's dancing sleeves
            for a while longer.

CHORUS   "Please protect my Yoshitsune!"
            she prays.
            It is truly moving.

kuse   *(shite dances to the chorus' song)*
CHORUS   When one thinks back on
            Kagetoki's slander of Yoshitsune,
            its source was the headwaters
            near the port of Watanabe,[18]
            where Kagetoki frivolously proposed
            installing "reverse oars"

---

[16]This *kuri* appears only in the Kita and Kongō school texts.

[17]The vow of Hachiman Daibosatsu that he will especially assist those who are honest. Quoted from section 6 of *Jikkinshō*.

[18]A port in Settsu province (now Osaka) whence Yoshitsune departed for the battle of Yashima.

in bow of the boat in case
the full tide turned against
them in the flow of battle.[19]
A cowardly, wavering suggestion.
(stamps and spreads arms)
Well, Yoshitsune has been upright
in all of his endeavors.
If there is truth in
(goes to front center stage)
the vow of the Yoshino god
to save those who are honest,
Yoritomo should reconsider
(goes to corner)
and Yoshitsune should receive
(large circle left to center back)
an Imperial order granting him
provinces southwest of the capital.
If this should happen,
all of you, monk-soldiers of
this temple, should proceed
to the capital and surrender to him.
Accept as well Yoshitsune's favors
on your pious sleeves.
With deep respect, I urge you:
Do not be disloyal to him.
(stamps at center back)
He won't hold a grudge against you.
(opens fan)

SHITE   Those among you, the monk-soldiers,

CHORUS   who bear deep anger toward him,
               even though you go forward and
               (goes forward and circles right)
               pursue him, it would be difficult
               to stop and kill Yoshitsune's
               redoubtable warriors, the famed

---

[19]This suggestion, to prepare for the possibility of retreat should the battle go against them, was scorned by Yoshitsune. Hence Kajiwara Kagetoki's resentment built up, and he later slandered Yoshitsune. The name Kajiwara contains the syllables *kaji*, which have a homonym meaning "oar"; hence this passage contains an elaborate set of words associated with oars: headwater, river's flow, and full tide. This tale is related in book 11 of the *Tale of the Heike* (Takagi 1966: 302-306; McCullough 1988: 358-60). See also *Yoshitsune* (McCullough, 1966, 32-34.)

> Kataoka, Mashio, Washio, and Tadanobu;
> they are unsurpassed soldiers!
> *(pauses at shite spot to point fan at waki)*
> Do not be the targets of the arrows
> *(goes to corner, raises fan, circles left)*
> they shoot in defense of their lord.
> So she spoke.
> Indeed, there is none
> among the monk-soldiers
> who would make a move.
> *(at center back performs small zigzag)*

waka   *(sits at shite spot)*
              "Serenely, gracefully,

jonomai   *(The shite rises. She stamps her feet to the drum beats
and dances quietly to the music. The dance is long, slow and graceful.)*

waka   *(shite raises fan, performs a small zigzag)*
SHITE   "Serenely, gracefully,
              I wind and rewind again,
              the yarn on my spool,

CHORUS   I wish there was a way
              of bringing back the past."[20]

noriji
CHORUS   Most of the soldiers
              entranced by her dance,
              most of the soldiers
              entranced by her dance,
              (shite goes to center front)
              allow time to pass,
              unwilling to stir.
              (spreads arms and looks intently)
              Or else, some soldiers, fearful of

---

[20]This is the song to which Shizuka danced before her enemy Yoritomo at Tsurugaoka Hachiman Shrine in Kamakura, defying him by saying that she wished to bring back the glorious past when Yoshitsune was at his height. See the story in McCullough 1966: 230-35. *Shizu ya shizu,* translated as "serenely, gracefully" puns on Shizuka's name. *Shizu* also refers to a type of weaving bobbin. The song alludes to a poem in the *Tales of Ise,* section 32 (McCullough 1968: 93)

(circles right to center stage)
Yoshitsune's bravery,
think to let him escape.
(sweeping her fan over them, shite looks around)
Eventually
(stamps)
time goes by
and thanks to Tadanobu's
(points fan at waki)
skillful plotting
(circles stage to shite spot)
his lord has made his escape
without difficultly.
(raises fan and makes small circle to left)
With her wish thus attained,
her mind serene
she returns to the capital,
(facing front, spreads her arms)
she returns to the capital.
(stamps to conclude play)

translated by H. Mack Horton

大江山

ŌEYAMA

CHARACTERS

Waki: Minamoto no Yorimitsu

Wakizure: (Warriors) Yasumasa, Sadamitsu, Suetake, Tsuna, Kintoki and The Peerless Warrior

Kyōgen: Yorimitsu's Servant and an abducted Woman

Shite
(act 1):   Shuten Dōji
(act 2):   Demon

Kokata: Two serving girls

SETTING: An autumn day during the Heian period at Ōeyama, a mountain in Tanba Province (Kyoto-fu). The historical brigands believed to have been eradicated by Yorimitsu resided at another Ōeyama (now called Oinosaka) within Kyoto city.

AUTHOR: Possibly by Miyamasu (Toita 1984), but there is no consensus.

148

CATEGORY: A fifth-category, demon play.

PERFORMANCE PRACTICES: Performed by all schools. The kokata do not always appear, and the number of wakizure varies.

TEXT: The translation is of the Kanze text in Sanari 1930-31: 1, 553-571. The Kita version (Nogami 1971: 5, 499-518) was consulted, and the Konparu version (*Kokuritsu Nogakudō* 1987: 10-11) provided *shōdan* divisions.

SOURCES: *Ōyama ekotoba* (late 14th century) and possibly an *otōgizoshi* entitled *Shuten dōji*.

ACKNOWLEDGEMENTS: The translator would like to thank Professor Horikoshi Zentarō of Tōkai University for helpful advice.

ŌEYAMA (The Demon of Ōeyama)

Translated by H. Mack Horton

ACT ONE

issei music (*The waki, Minamoto Yorimitsu, enters wearing the small cap and unlined surplice of a mountain ascetic, together with a small-sleeved, brocade kimono and white divided skirts under a travel cloak bound with a narrow sash. He has a short sword, a fan, and a rosary. The wakizure warriors accompanying him are similarly attired, and the kyōgen servant wears a mountain ascetic's cap and surplice, a small-sleeved, brocade kimono tucked in trousers with leggings. He has a short sword and a fan and enters last, stopping at the kyōgen spot.*)

issei WAKI & WAKIZURE	(*facing each other at stage front*) Westward with the sound of the autumn wind course clouds and the West River, wending their way toward the peak of Ōeyama.[1]
nanori WAKI	(*facing front*) I am Minamoto no Yorimitsu.[2]
sashi	In keeping with an oracle, Yasumasa[3] and Yorimitsu have been bidden to subdue

---

[1]West River refers to the Katsura River flowing through Tanba province, west of the capital. The autumn wind was believed to blow westward.

[2]Minamoto (no) Yorimitsu (also read Raikō, 948-1021), son of Mitsunaka, was a warrior aristocrat, poet, provincial governor, and famous archer. He appears in various martial *setsuwa* tales, in the noh plays *Tsuchigumo* and *Rashōmon*, and in a group of puppet and kabuki plays called "Raikōmono."

[3]Hirai Yasumasa (also read Hōshō, 958-1036) was an aristocrat of Fujiwara lineage, poet, governor of Tango province, and husband of the poet Izumi Shikibu (see note 16). He also figures in *setsuwa* tales and in the noh play *Rashōmon*.

150

the demon that dwells
on Ōeyama in
Tanba province.

WAKIZURE   Yorimitsu and Yasumasa
wondered how we might
even with our many men
manage to vanquish
a fiend of inhuman form.

WAKI   But then striking on a plan,
we attired ourselves
in mountain-ascetic garb.

WAKIZURE   We wear in place of helmets
these monkish caps;

WAKI   hempen surplices, not armor;

WAKIZURE   wooden packs, not weapons.

WAKI   Thus garbed are Yorimitsu
and Yasumasa,

WAKIZURE   Sadamitsu, Suetake,
Tsuna, Kintoki,[4]

PEERLESS   And also the renowned
Peerless Warrior,[5]

WAKIZURE   fifty men and more in all.

WAKI   While it is still night,

ageuta   *(facing each other)*
WAKI &   we leave the capital beneath

[4]Known as the "Four Heavenly Kings of Yorimitsu" (*Raikō shitennō*), these men are all mentioned in the noh play *Rashōmon*. Usui Sadamitsu (n.d.) and Urabe Suetake (c. 950-1022) are of Taira lineage; Watanabe Tsuna (953-1024/5) was raised by the brother-in-law of Yorimitsu, and Sakata Kintoki (n.d.) was an orphan Yorimitsu is said to have rescued from poverty.

[5]*Hitorimusha*, known only in legend as a retainer of Yasumasa. He is the waki in the noh play *Tsuchigumo*.

WAKIZURE   the late-rising moon,
we leave the capital beneath
the late-rising moon.
Presently we find that we
have reached West River;
the wind and waves rise up,
wave-white the sacred strips
for the blessing that sustains us.
Secure in the thought
that whether demon or no,
none can evade
(waki takes steps to indicate travel)
the will of our great sovereign,
we press onward and
reach the foot-wearying mountain
of Ōeyama,
reach the foot-wearying mountain
of Ōeyama.

tsukizerifu
WAKI   Having hastened on our way, we have reached Ōeyama. Here we will inquire of the dwelling of the Dōji and take our lodging.

WAKIZURE   It is well for us to do so.

(All go to the bridgeway. At the first pine the waki turns to face the servant kyōgen.)

WAKI   Servant!

SERVANT   What is your bidding?

WAKI   Inquire here of the place where the Dōji dwells and find lodging for us.

SERVANT   As you command.

(The waki and wakizure rest facing the back wall of the bridgeway while the servant stands at the shite spot.)

mondō
SERVANT   Such a dreadful task I have been given! A fearsome

thing it is to lead the way to a demon's den.   I must make haste!

(As he makes a circlet, the woman kyōgen wearing a female cap, small-sleeved kimono and sash, enters through the small, side door carrying an embroidered kimono.   In the back corner she begins to mime washing clothes.)

SERVANT   How deep this valley and how steep and treacherous the path!   Wait--how strange!   Why should there be blood flowing in this stream?   *(looks at the woman)* A demon must have turned himself into that woman washing clothes.   How sinister!   And yet, she looks like someone I have seen in the capital.   I'll have a word with her.

WOMAN   Such a dreadful task!   Over and over I'm made to wash blood-soaked garments.   What could be more pitiful!

SERVANT   My lady!   *(approaches the woman who looks up at him)*

WOMAN   Are you addressing me?   Why have you come here?

SERVANT   I have come for good reason.   First tell my why you are here.

WOMAN   I was abducted by Shuten Dōji over three years ago. Since then I have washed clothes such as these day in and day out.

SERVANT   I see.   I serve Lord Yorimitsu who has come to quell the Dōji.   We will take you back to the capital, so will you request lodging for us?

WOMAN   If you will take me back to the capital, I'll find a place for you to stay.   Please wait there while I speak to the Dōji.

SERVANT   Certainly.

(The servant sits down, and the woman goes to the first pine and faces the curtain.)

mondō
WOMAN   I would address the Dōji.

(The shite, Shuten Dōji, enters wearing a dōji mask, a large black headpiece with a white headband, an unpatterned short-sleeved kimono and a red divided skirt under a brocade kimono tucked up at the waist. He is followed by two kokata, girl servants, in women's wigs with hairbands, silver-leaf small-sleeved kimono, and brocade kimono wrapped as skirts. They all carry fans.)

SHITE   Who is it that calls the Dōji?

WOMAN   Some mountain ascetics have arrived and ask a night's lodgings.

SHITE   What? A night's lodging for ascetics? Most regrettable! When I left Mount Hiei at the order of Emperor Kanmu, I firmly vowed to leave monks alone.[6] Show them to the corridor near the middle gate.
               (sits on a stool on the bridgeway)

mondō   *(woman returns to stage)*
WOMAN   Are you there, sir?

SERVANT   Here I am.

WOMAN   I conveyed your request to the Dōji, and he said you might use the corridor near the middle gate. Please come this way.

SERVANT   Certainly.

(The woman goes to sit behind the musicians, and the servant moves towards the waki.)

SERVANT   My lord, I requested lodging, and they said we might use the corridor near the middle gate. Please come this way.

[6]Mount Hiei is located northeast of Kyoto city, the direction from which demons were believed to enter. Emperor Kanmu (737-806), founder of the Nagaoka and Heian capitals, attended ceremonies at Dengyō daishi's temple on Mount Hiei in 794 (see footnote 9).

(The waki and wakizure return to the stage and sit in a crescent between the waki spot and back center stage.   The shite also enters and sits on a stool at center stage.)

mondō

SHITE   Travelling monks!   Where did you come from and where are you bound, to have ventured on my hidden dwelling?

WAKI   We are from Mount Hiko in Tsukushi.[7] We lost our way on the Sennondo road at the foot of this mountain and have been wandering in confusion.[8] We are most grateful for your lodging us this evening. Why, might I ask, are you known as Shuten Dōji?

SHITE   My retainers call me Shuten Dōji, the Wine-Drinking Lad, because I drink wine day and night. Nothing I have seen or heard pleases me like wine. Travelling monks--join me in a cup!

(The kokata stand to pour for the waki and wakizure.)

WAKI   As you wish. *(accepts wine from the kokata)*
       How long have you been residing on this mountain?

SHITE   My ancestral home was on Mount Hiei, and I lived there many years, but then that charlatan, the Great Teacher Dengyō, built his temple, the Konponchūdō, at the peak and the Seven Shrines at the foot.[9] Mortified, I displayed my wondrous powers by turning myself overnight into a camphor tree more than 300 feet tall, but the priest composed this poem:

---

[7]A mountain in Fukuoka prefecture traditionally held sacred by mountain ascetics. Tsukushi is the ancient name for Kyushu.

[8]The San'indō, one of the major arteries of pre-modern Japan, going along the Japan Sea side of what is now western Honshu.

[9]Dengyō Daishi (also known as Saichō, 767-822), founder of the Tendai Sect of Buddhism in Japan and of its main temple, Enryakuji, on Mt. Hiei. The Konponchūdō, first built in 788, is its central structure. The Seven Shrines are actually three groups of seven shrines each, which comprise the Hie Shrine complex on the Ōtsu side of the mountain.

I beseech the Buddhas
of supreme wisdom, perfect
    and all pervasive,
to grant divine protection
to the mountain where I stand.[10]

The Buddhas were deceived by the priest and drove
me out. I was powerless and so left Hiei, the mountain that had been my home for ages.

WAKI   So you left Hiei and
            came here straight away?

SHITE   No. I then wandered aimless,
            hiding in the haze,
            and riding upon the clouds.

WAKI   You journeyed down the long road
            through the countryside,
            rustic places distant as
            the far-flung firmament?

SHITE   I saw Tsukushi as well,
            land you call your home.

WAKI   There is nowhere you have not been,
            East, west, north, or south
            in this sub-celestial realm.

SHITE   Treading a path across the sky,

WAKI   now at Mt. Hiko,

SHITE   now Mt. Dai in Hōki,[11]

[10]*Shinkokinshū* poem 1921 by Dengyō. The poem bears the heading "On the construc-
tion of the [Konpon]chūdō on Mt. Hiei."

[11]A mountain in Hōki province (western Tottori prefecture), sometimes called the "Fuji
of Hōki," which serves as a center for mountain asceticism.

WAKI	Shirayama Tateyama, and the sacred peak of Fuji,[12]
SHITE	to the moon in the heavens,
WAKI	then returning on a path that leads through the clouds,
SHITE	like one still drawn by the wheel of transmigration.
WAKI	to this place that is hard by the capital city,
SHITE	Oeyama mountain, where I am sequestered,
WAKI	in your secret, secret home.
SHITE	Dwelling here concealed, I am now revealed by you travelling monks, and my mystical powers weaken.
WAKI	Be of serene mind, for we will not reveal you.
SHITE	How happy I am! I implore you not to do so. "Taking shelter neath the same tree
WAKI	or drinking from the same stream," just so our meeting.[13] Our priestly hearts are founded on benevolence,

[12]Shirayama, also read Hakusan, is at the border of Ishikawa and Gifu prefectures; Tateyama is in Toyama prefecture. All three mountains are associated with mountain worship and asceticism.

[13]A Buddhist proverb which concludes "even these are bonds from a former life," i.e., even the most ephemeral encounters are predestined by the law of cause and effect.

SHITE   and your appearance proclaims
                your devotion to
                the salvation of mankind.

WAKI   True, we are of monkish guise.

SHITE   I was likewise raised upon
                the holy mountain.

WAKI   There can be no doubt that you
                are of boyish mien,

SHITE   So bestow your kindness on me!

WAKI   Even the gods come second.

uta
CHORUS   "First the temple youths,
                then the Mountain King"--
                monks hold the temple boys much dearer
                than they do the gods themselves![14]
                Since you are priest and I, a lad,
                can you but show me kindness?
                Do come away and favor me
                with your conversation.

*(The shite reaches out to the waki with his left hand and beckons
silently, then, during the following song, rises and dances.)*

ageuta
CHORUS   "At the Black Mound of
                Adachigahara moor,
                at the Black Mound of
                Adachigahara moor,
                in the distant north
                a demon is said to dwell";
                it is true, so true![15]

[14]A proverb meaning here that the monks of Mt. Hiei pay more attention to the temple
boys than to reverence owed the deity of the Hie Shrine. A reference to monastic sexual proclivities.

[15]The Black Mound (Kurozuka) is in Fukushima prefecture and is the locale of the noh
play *Kurozuka*. The poem is *Shūishū* 559 by Taira Kanemori labelled "Sent on hearing that

But not so Ōeyama,
sung of in such songs as
"far is the way past
Ōeyama mountain
and Ikuta Field,"
and linked with Yosa Bay and
the Bridge of Heaven.[16]
Know that even the *tengu*
of Ōeyama mountain
is a friend of mine.[17]

sageuta   *(sits facing the waki)*
CHORUS   Come, let us drink, let us drink.

(The waki stands, pours for the shite then returns to the waki spot. The shite accepts the wine, then dances to the following song.)

dan no uta
CHORUS   What will go well with the wine?
Among the flowers
Of the autumn mountains
there are pampas grass,
bell flowers, burnets, and asters--
and who was it that
nicknamed asters "demons' weed?"

SHITE   *(opens his fan)*
Indeed, it is true,

CHORUS   indeed, it is true
that Demons' Castle is near,

Shigeyuki had younger sisters at Kurozuka in Natori, Michinoku." In the original poem, the last line is a question: "but would that indeed be true?" The poem also appears in *Yamato monogatari* 58.

[16]Ikuno is south of Ōeyama mountain. The poem is *Kin'yōshū* 550 by Koshikibu no Naishi, Izumi Shikibu's daughter, and it also appears in *Hyakunin isshu*. The poem was written in response to a challenge that perhaps she had had to send to Tango where her mother was living to obtain an entry for a poetry contest. The last two lines of the original are "so I have seen no letter/nor crossed the Bridge of Heaven." The play recasts the meaning and includes the Bay of Yosa which surrounds the Bridge of Heaven (Ama no hashidate), one of the Three Famous Sights of Japan.

[17]Tengu are mythical winged creatures thought to live in mountains and to dress like mountain ascetics, with whom they are often associated.

at the border of
Tango and Tanba.[18]
I am safe! Secure!
(takes two steps and raises his fan twice)
I have drunk cup after cup;
would my face be flushed?
Do not dream I am a demon;
it is the wine that makes me red.
If you could but come to know me
(goes toward the waki spot)
and not be so afraid,
you would find that I can be
an entertaining friend!
(gestures towards himself)
I too was filled with fear
when I first set eyes on you,
(looks toward waki)
when I first set eyes on you.
But now that I know you better,
I think you are very nice![19]
(beckons to waki with fan, then kneels)

ageuta   Round and round go the cups,
time and time again.
(extends fan to accept wine from wakizure then stands)
The sky of dawn is also
"drunk with the blossoms."[20]
(lifts fan above his head)
His feet uncertain,
(staggers backwards and sits crosslegged)
floating and drifting,
(kokata help him stand)
gathering up clouds
and spreading them beneath him,

---

[18]Demons' Castle (Onigajō) is a mountain in Kyoto prefecture southeast of Ōeyama, which was believed to be the home of Ibaraki Dōji, a henchmen of Shuten Dōji and the demon in early modern versions of the tale treated in the noh *Rashōmon*. The suggestion here is that the asters owe their nickname to their proximity to Demons' Castle.

[19]This passage, beginning with "Would my face be flushed," later appears as a *yamatobushi* in the *Kanginshū* (190), a medieval anthology of popular songs.

[20]*Wakan rōeishū* 39 by Sugawara Michizane. Upon the third day of/the last month of springtime/ the sky is drunk with the blossoms/of the peaches and damsons now at their height.

he retires to his unseen
(shite goes to bridgeway)
Demon's Den.   Opening
the Screen of Angry Waves,[21]
(shite mimes opening door and exits)
he enters his bedchamber,
he enters his bedchamber.

mondō   *(waki watches him leave, then stands at the shite spot*
                facing the servant)
WAKI   Servant!

SERVANT   What is your bidding?

WAKI   Obtain by stealth the key to the Dōji's bedchamber.

SERVANT   As you command.
                (waki and wakizure exit)

INTERLUDE

mondō   *(servant stands at shite spot)*
SERVANT   Are you there, my lady?

WOMAN   *(goes to waki spot)*   Here I am.

SERVANT   Did you give the key to Yorimitsu?

WOMAN   I did indeed.

SERVANT   Good.   Now then, Yorimitsu said that at times like
                these women are a hindrance and that I was to take
                you ahead with me to the capital.   Isn't that splen-
                did?

[21]"Unseen demon" (*me ni mienu oni*) is a phrase from the Japanese Preface to the *Kokin-shū*. The emperor's living quarters in the imperial palace (*seiryōden*) has a Demon's Den (*oni no ma*) and a standing screen called the Screen of Angry Waves (*araumi no shōji*).

WOMAN   Oh yes, it's wonderful!

SERVANT   Then let's be off.   Come along.

WOMAN   I'm coming.

(The two walk in a large circle.)

SERVANT   You are most fortunate.

WOMAN   I am, to be sure.

SERVANT   And what's more, since you helped us find lodging, there will certainly be a reward for you when my lord returns to the capital.

WOMAN   I wish for no reward.   Nothing could make me happier than returning to the capital and seeing my husband and my child.

SERVANT   I understand completely.   But I doubt you will be going home.

WOMAN   How so?

SERVANT   Since you were abducted by the Dōji, a pretty young lady took your place.   They ignore the child and are getting along so well together I am envious.

WOMAN   Infuriating!   He has taken a new wife?

SERVANT   He didn't know if you were alive or dead, and he was not to be without a wife.

WOMAN   I don't mind his taking another, but it's sad that they ignore the child.

SERVANT   If I might make a suggestion?

WOMAN   Of course.

SERVANT   Because I led the way to the Demon's Den, Lord Yorimitsu will probably give me a reward as well when he returns to the capital.   And he will likely give one to you. We will both be able to live comfortably. As it happens, I have no wife. Why don't you be my wife?

WOMAN   Impossible! How could I, with a child?

SERVANT   Even if you see it as your duty, you can't go back. Please, be my wife.

WOMAN   Well, if that's how things are, I will.

SERVANT   Excellent! The capital is already close by. Let's make haste.

WOMAN   I'm coming.

SERVANT   Stay with me for a thousand years, ten thousand years.

WOMAN   I will, I will. *(they exit)*

ACT TWO

(The stage attendants place a straw mat dais at back center stage with a covered frame on it to suggest a room.)

ashirai drum music   *(The waki and wakizure enter. They have removed their mountain ascetic caps, surplices and travel cloaks, and put on white headbands and long swords. The waki holds a torch.   They line up on the bridgeway.)*

sashi
WAKI   Already the night is late
                         and the sky, pitch dark;
                         darker still, the demon's lair.
                         We open the iron gate

(He approaches the stage and, facing the stage prop, mimes opening a door.)

and peer inside. How strange!
What had looked before
like a human form is now

ageuta   *(lifts his torch and peers in)*
CHORUS   twenty feet in height!
twenty feet in height!
Though the demon sleeps
the spectacle is daunting.
(throws down torch, goes to shite spot)
But we came resolved
for the sake of our sovereign
(makes an obeisance to the front)
and our divine land.
We invoke its deities,
naming above all
Hachiman and the avatar
of the Mountain King,
asking them to grant us strength.[22]
(faces the warriors on the bridgeway)
Raikō, Hōshō,
Tsuna, Kintoki,
Sadamitsu, Suetake,
and the Peerless Warrior
stand joined of purpose.

(The waki goes to the waki spot and faces the stage prop. As their names are called the wakizure enter the stage. The Peerless Warrior goes to the corner, the others line up behind the waki. All face the stage prop.)

kuri   Over the sleeping demon
our flying swords flash--
as mighty as lightning and
the roar of thunder.

(The cloth covering of the stage prop is let down to reveal the shite crouched inside, looking down and holding a small-sleeved kimono as a coverlet over his head and shoulders. He wears a shikami demon mask, red headpiece, gold brocade headband, a small-

---

[22]Hachiman was the clan deity of the Minamoto.

sleeved, brocade kimono under a happi cloak and broad, patterned divided skirts.   He holds a demon's stick.)

mondō
SHITE   Oh travelling monks, you have
                   disappointed me!
                   You said that you spoke the truth.
                   For my part I know
                   "Demons do not stray from the
                   path of righteousness."[23]

(He lifts his coverlet, looks at the waki, then looks down again.   The Peerless Warrior brandishes his sword.)

PEERLESS   What?   Did you say "Demons do not stray from the
                   path of righteousness?"

SHITE   Just so.

PEERLESS   Nay, you lie!   Why then do you
                   foment chaos while
                   living in our sovereign's realm?
                   Why abduct his subjects?
                   No doubt you have heard of me,
                   the Peerless Warrior,
                   in Yasumasa's service.
                   Demon though you are,
                   you will never elude us,
                   all the more because
                   we act at our monarch's will.
jōnoei   "Even the earth and trees
                   are a part of the domain
                   of our great sovereign.
                   Where then could a place be found
                   for demons like you to dwell?"[24]

CHORUS   Let him not escape!
                   Let him not slip past!
                   Attack him!   Attack!

---

[23]A proverb of unknown origins.

[24] A slight variation on a poem in the *Taiheiki* (Chapter 16), by Ki no Tomō.

(waki and Peerless Warrior face each other)
With their blades as one,
they fall upon him.

noriji   *(draw their swords and stand facing demon)*
CHORUS   The mountains and rivers,
grasses and trees tremble;
the mountains and rivers,
grasses and trees tremble.
(the shite stands)
The eyes of the demon flash,
(throws off his coverlet)
blazing with a light
like the sun, the moon, the stars.
Who could face him?

maibataraki (The shite steps down from the dais and dances.   The shite crosses weapons with the waki and wakizure, then remounts the dais and, brandishing his stick, faces the waki.   The waki and wakizure face him with their swords raised.)

noriji
WAKI   But Raikō and Hōshō,

CHORUS   but Raikō and Hōshō
of course have no fear,
for whether demon or no,
with Yorimitsu's skill
how could anything escape?
He dashes forward
seizes the demon's arm, and
they grapple fiercely.
(shite and waki cross weapons)
Eiya! they now contend
with all of their might.
Yorimitsu is forced down,
but at the moment
when he is to be devoured,
(shite brandishes his stick and glares)
he draws his short sword
and from beneath runs him through
again and again!
(waki stabs at shite)

All his force behind his sword,
he flings him over,

(The shite   brandishes his stick, then subsides, sitting crosslegged.)

Then pressing down the demon,
of late so mighty,
he strikes off his angry head.

(The waki strikes the shite who exits via the side door. The waki then shoulders his sword at the shite spot and performs the concluding stamps to the following words.)

Thereafter all descended
Ōeyama mountain
and then departed homeward
for the capital.

BŌSHIBARI

棒縛

translated by Eileen Katō

CHARACTERS

Shite: Jirōkaja

Ado: Tarōkaja

Ado: The Master

SETTING: A household in medieval Japan.

AUTHOR: Unknown

CATEGORY: Classified as a *shōmyō* (literally, "small name") piece. In this group of plays Tarōkaja is usually played by the shite, although here the role goes to Jirōkaja.

170

PERFORMANCE PRACTICES: Many variations exist.   In the
             Izumi school the Master gets the upper hand.

TEXT: Based on the Ōkura text as performed at the Na-
             tional Noh Theater, November 11, 1983, on the
             occasion of Mrs. Nancy Reagan's visit.

TRANSLATIONS: English, Bōshibari 1882: 353-361, McKinnon 1968: 13-26,
             Kenny 1989: 37-48; French, Seiffert 1979: 1,326-338.

BŌSHIBARI (Tied to a Stick)

Translated by Eileen Katō

A PLAY IN ONE ACT

(The master comes on followed by his two manservants, Tarōkaja and Jirōkaja. All three are clad in matched vests and long trailing trousers. The master's undergarment is striped, the servants' checked. The master, carrying a short sword, goes to the shite spot, and the two servants sit in the back area.)

MASTER
: I am a man that lives in these parts. I have to go across that hill over there on a bit of business. Now it happens that every time I have to go away like this, my two rascally servants take advantage of my absence to steal and drink my saké, but today, I'll fix them! I'll tie them up good and tight before I leave. And now I'll call in Tarōkaja and have a little chat with him. Ho ho Tarōkaja! Are you there?
(goes to waki spot)

TARŌKAJA
: YEEAAH...!
(getting up)
At your orders, Sir.
(comes to shite spot)

MASTER
: Aha! So you were there!

TARŌKAJA
: Here I am before you!

MASTER
: And faster than I expected. If I've called you it is for this and nothing else--for reasons best known to myself, I want you to tie up Jirōkaja for me.

TARŌKAJA
: Oh, Sir! I don't know what he's been up to or what he's done to you, but for this time Sir! oh, please spare him!

172

MASTER No, No. It's only for a little while and won't do him a bit of harm. However this Jirōkaja is a wily trickster and if you seem to be saying 'Here I come! I'm going to get you!', he's not just going to stay there and let you catch him. So, what's to be done?

TARŌKAJA Yes indeed! What am I going to do? Oh! I've thought of a good way. Lately the fellow has been taking lessons in stick-fencing. Now he's learned a secret move he's very proud of, called 'warding off a night attack'. You'll ask him to demonstrate this for you and when he is in the middle of it, we'll pounce and tie him to his stick. What do you say to that, Sir?

MASTER Splendid! That's a capital idea. Now, go and call in Jirōkaja!

TARŌKAJA At your service, Sir!
(takes a few steps in Jirōkaja's direction)
Ho Ho! Jirōkaja! The Master wants you.
(Jirōkaja gets up)

JIRŌKAJA What! He wants me?

TARŌKAJA Exactly.

JIRŌKAJA If he wants me, why doesn't he say so himself?

TARŌKAJA Come on! Stop dawdling!

JIRŌKAJA Oh, all right!
(goes to shite spot; Tarōkaja steps back)

JIRŌKAJA Here I am, Sir! At your service!

MASTER And faster than I expected. If I've called you, it is for this and nothing else--I've heard that lately you've been taking lessons in stick-fencing. Isn't that so? I'd like you to demonstrate for me a feint or two.

JIRŌKAJA Oh no, Sir! I don't do anything like that at all.

MASTER   Come, come.   None of your lies now!   'Twas
             Tarōkaja that told me.

JIRŌKAJA   What!   You went and told him?

TARŌKAJA   Exactly!   I went and told him, and now, just go
             ahead and show him how it's done.

JIRŌKAJA   *(facing Master)*
             Oh well, if Bigmouth has told you, I might as well
             go ahead and show you how it's done.

MASTER   You'd do well to do just that!

JIRŌKAJA   First of all, I must get my stick.

MASTER   Quick then.   Go and get it!

JIRŌKAJA   At your orders!

TARŌKAJA   Come on!   Come on!   Go and get it, quick!

(Jirōkaja goes to fetch stick from back of stage)

MASTER   *(to Tarōkaja)*
             You'll give me a signal when it's the right time!

TARŌKAJA   At your orders!

(Jirōkaja returns with stick)

JIRŌKAJA   Please, Sir!   Beg your pardon, Sir!   This is the stick.

MASTER   Oh, so that's the stick?

JIRŌKAJA   *(miming the actions described)*
             Now first, if you're attacked from in front, you
             parry like this.   That'll make the other fellow raise
             the sword he has lowered.   The minute he lifts it,
             you're ready to rush in and sock him one in the
             midriff, and when you see him double up, you'll
             land him a right good wallop on the shins!   Perfectly
             simple!

MASTER   'Pon my word, but that was beautifully executed!

TARŌKAJA   Aye, and bravely too!

MASTER   There was a feint or something called...what was it?
              Oh, you know!

JIRŌKAJA   Not another thing do I know, Sir!

MASTER   No, No, none of that now!   What's this it's called?
              Oh yes!   I've got it!   Show me how you go about
              'warding off a night attack'!

JIRŌKAJA   *(To Tarōkaja)*
              And did you have to spill the beans about 'warding
              off a night attack'?

TARŌKAJA   Sure!   I told him all about it, so now show him!

JIRŌKAJA   But that's my secret trick!   However, since Tarōkaja
              couldn't keep his big mouth shut, I'll show you how
              it's done.
              (Goes to front center stage)
              Now when decent folk like you and me go on an
              errand in the middle of the night, we risk having
              our money-belts robbed; but if only I have my
              stick, I don't have a thing to fear.

MASTER   Oh ho!

JIRŌKAJA   So what we call 'warding off a night attack' consists
              in this!
              *(puts the stick behind the back of his neck along his
              shoulders, and holds it with his outstretched arms)*
              If I'm attacked on my left, I parry like this!   If I'm
              Attacked on my right, I parry like that!   In a word,
              I watch and ward before and behind, and I fear
              nothing and nobody!
              (moves forward a little)

MASTER   *(Coming up behind him)*
& TARŌ   You rascally rogue, you're no match for us!
              (each ties one of Jirōkaja's wrists to the stick)

JIRŌKAJA   What on earth did you do that for?

MASTER   Why did I do that?   But surely, you can guess!

JIRŌKAJA   No!   I haven't the faintest!   And *you*, Tarōkaja!
Why would you do a thing like that to your own
best friend?!

TARŌKAJA   Must obey orders, you know!   Must obey orders!

MASTER   Hee!   Hi!   Ho!   Hum!   And that's that, all nicely
& TARŌ   settled!

*(They propel Jirōkaja toward the waki spot; Tarōkaja stands with
his hands behind his back and jeers.)*

TARŌKAJA   Oh my! you look great like that!   Oh, but you do
look great!

MASTER   You wretch!

(He pounces and quickly ties Tarōkaja's hands behind his back.)

TARŌKAJA   Hey! what am I to blame for?   Nothing, I'm sure!

MASTER   Oh, come, come!   You too must have an idea!

TARŌKAJA   No, not the slightest inkling!

JIRŌKAJA   Oh my! you look great like that!   Oh, but you do
look great!   Good for you, Master!   Tie him up good
and tight now!

MASTER   Hee!   Hi!   Ho!   Hum!   And that's that, all nicely
settled!
(propels Tarōkaja to the corner)
Fine!   Fine!   And now, pay good heed to me, the
two of you!   I have to go across the hill over there
on a bit of business and you two--mind the house
while I'm away!

JIRŌKAJA   What!   How can we mind the house if we're trussed
up like this?

TARŌKAJA   A robber could come in and I wouldn't even know it!

MASTER   I'm off now!

JIRŌKAJA   Please Master!

TARŌKAJA   Master!

JIRŌKAJA   Master!

TARŌKAJA   Master!

JIRŌKAJA   Do you know? I think he's already gone!

TARŌKAJA   You're right, I'm sure! I think he's already gone!

JIRŌKAJA   Good! Come on over here!

TARŌKAJA   Right!

JIRŌKAJA   *(go to back center stage and sit)*
& TARŌ   Hee! Hi! Ho! Hum! Well now, that's done!

JIRŌKAJA   Now why do you think the two of us got tied up like this today? That's what I'd like to know!

TARŌKAJA   Yes indeed! Why were we tied up like this? That's what I'd like to know!

JIRŌKAJA   If you want my opinion, it's because every time he leaves the house, we steal and drink his saké. That's what he's tied us up for.

TARŌKAJA   You've got it! It's surely for something like that.

JIRŌKAJA   Hey, what do you think? When you're tied up like this, doesn't it give you a terrible thirst for saké?

TARŌKAJA   Now you've said something! Thinking that I can't have it makes me thirstier than ever for a drop of saké!

JIRŌKAJA   We've got to find a way to open the cellar door!

TAROKAJA   I couldn't agree with you more, but how are we to go about it?

JIROKAJA   Ha! I've got it! Here, look! *(moves his hands)* My hands are free! I'll see if I can't slide open the cellar door.

TAROKAJA   But how will you manage to do it, tied up like that?

JIROKAJA   Just wait a minute!
(gets up and moves forward)
Oh, I hope it's going to open!

TAROKAJA   That's it! Let's keep hoping anyway that it's going to open!

(Jirōkaja lowers his right hand and mimes pushing open a sliding door, hopping sideways with it)

JIROKAJA   Garari! Garari! Garari garari! Garari garari garari! Easy does it! There we are! It's open all the way!

TAROKAJA   Not a word of lie! It's open all the way!

JIROKAJA   Oh, goody, goody! Just get an eyeful of that! It's full of casks!

TAROKAJA   Why, you're telling the truth!

JIROKAJA   Well now, which cask are we going to broach?

TAROKAJA   I leave it to you to choose one to your taste.

JIROKAJA   Well now, how's that? We're in luck! Here's a cask with the top already unsealed. Let's try this one!

TAROKAJA   A marvelous idea you've just had there!

JIROKAJA   And now let me lift off the cover! Hee! Hi! Ho! Hum! and there we are!
(Mimes lifting off the cover)
Mmmm! How sweet it smells! Mmmmmmm!

TAROKAJA   I can smell it from here even.

JIRŌKAJA   And now I must get something to ladle it out with.

TARŌKAJA   Oh! do hurry up and get something!

JIRŌKAJA   Right!   *(He goes to the back of the stage and fetches a large lacquered box-lid.)*
Heigh ho!   Heigh ho!   I've just got the right thing for ladling it out.   I'll tell you what, I'll draw some and give it to you to drink.

TARŌKAJA   You do that!   I'd be very much obliged to you!
(mimes drawing off the saké)

JIRŌKAJA   And there we are!   Come now, drink your fill!

TARŌKAJA   All right!   I'll have a little drink!

JIRŌKAJA   Drink quick!   *(Jirōkaja goes to Tarōkaja and kneels, holding the container at Tarōkaja's mouth level)*
There now, that's it!

TARŌKAJA   Oh me, oh my! but this is marvelous saké!

JIRŌKAJA   That I can well believe!   And now I'm going to draw some more, but this time, I'll drink it myself.

TARŌKAJA   Good idea!

JIRŌKAJA   *(drawing off saké)*   There we are!   And now let me drink!

TARŌKAJA   Marvelous idea!

JIRŌKAJA   If only I can manage to drink it!
(tries in vain to reach his mouth with the lacquer lid)
Heigh ho!   Here we go!   But what's this?   What's this!   It's all spilling over.   Ha! but this time will do the trick!   *(tries once more)*
No good!   It's all spilling over.

TARŌKAJA   And that's a fact!   It's all spilling over!

JIRŌKAJA   Too bad, but I'll have to let you drink what's left of this round too!

TARŌKAJA   You'll let me drink again?

JIRŌKAJA   Sure! *(repeats earlier mime)*   There we are!   There we are!

TARŌKAJA   Yum!   Yum!   Do you know what!   The more I drink, the better it gets!

JIRŌKAJA   I don't doubt that!   But I must say, I've had nearly enough of giving you drinks and not being able to drink at all myself!   I'll have to think of something!

TARŌKAJA   Yes, and indeed it is not much fun for a man to be the only one drinking, either.   I'd give anything to find a way to let you drink too.   Aha!   I've got it! I've got it!   I've just had the cleverest idea!   Draw off another lid-full.

JIRŌKAJA   What do you have in mind?

TARŌKAJA   Just go ahead and draw off the saké!

JIRŌKAJA   Right!   There we are!   Well, now it's drawn off, so what do I do next?

TARŌKAJA   *(getting up and turning his back)* Good!   That's fine! Now put it in my hands!   *(waggles his hands behind his back)*

JIRŌKAJA   Aha!   I see!   A neat trick that!   *(gives Tarokaja the lid)* And now let me at it!   *(gets on his knees, his mouth to the lid)*

TARŌKAJA   Quick now!   Drink up!

JIRŌKAJA   Right!

TARŌKAJA   There we are!   There we are!

JIRŌKAJA   Oh, goody, goody!   This is the best saké I've ever had in my life!   Let me draw off some more!

TARŌKAJA   How about giving us a little song?

JIRŌKAJA   Right you are!

(He sings while continuing to dip in the cask.   This song is of the actor's choosing and may be ad libbed.[1])

TARŌKAJA   Bravo!   Good man!   Bravo!

JIRŌKAJA   Oh, but we're having a glorious booze!

TARŌKAJA   You can say that again!

JIRŌKAJA   Well, I've done my bit! Now it's your turn to do your party piece!

TARŌKAJA   How can I do my party piece all tied up like this? Please, let me off this time!

JIRŌKAJA   Oh no, none of that now!   You'll only be all the funnier for being tied up.   How about a dance! Please!

TARŌKAJA   So you want me to dance, eh?

JIRŌKAJA   I'd be delighted if you would.

TARŌKAJA   *(dances while bawling out)*
'And when your turn is over,
Then you'd best be running home
Or your nurse'll get the blame...'

JIRŌKAJA   Bravo!   First class!   Bravo!

TARŌKAJA   Well, I've danced my dance!

JIRŌKAJA   To reward you for your trouble, I'm going to give you a drink!

TARŌKAJA   You'll give me another drink?

---

[1]The song may be lines from a noh play. Koyama suggests that lines from *Ukon* are often sung here (Koyama 1960: 310).

JIRŌKAJA   *(repeating earlier mime)* And there we are! And there we are!

TARŌKAJA   Oh! It's a fact! This saké here, the more you drink the better it gets!

JIRŌKAJA   I must draw off some more!

TARŌKAJA   Give us a bar!

JIRŌKAJA   Right!

(He draws off saké and sings; again this is a song of the actor's choice and may be ad libbed.[2])

TARŌKAJA   Bravo! Bravo! Bravo! The more we sing the merrier we get!

JIRŌKAJA   What a jolly booze we're having!

TARŌKAJA   The greatest! But I've done my bit. Now it's your turn to dance.

JIRŌKAJA   How do you expect me to dance, drawn and quartered as I am? Please let me off this time!

TARŌKAJA   Come on now, none of that! With you pulled every which way like that, it'll be all the more fun!

JIRŌKAJA   All right! So be it! Tell you what! I'll dance and you'll sing! How about that?

TARŌKAJA   Great!

JIRŌKAJA   *(dancing and bawling)*
              'A nice little girl
              Of sixteen or seventeen
              Is mighty sweet when taking down
              The washing off the pole;
              And she is even sweeter
              When she's rolling up the clothes;

[2]Lines from the noh play *Sakuragawa* are often chosen (Koyama 1960: 312).

But she is never half so sweet
As when I have my arms around
Her teeny weeny waist.....'

TARŌKAJA   Bravo! Bravo! Encore!

JIRŌKAJA   I have to admit that I wasn't at my most graceful!

TARŌKAJA   No matter! I think that calls for a drink to reward
you for your trouble! Here, put it in my hands!
(stands up)

JIRŌKAJA   You want to stand me another drink?

TARŌKAJA   Exactly! *(repeats his earlier mime)* And there we
are! And there we are!

JIRŌKAJA   Oh, it's a fact for sure! The more you drink the
better it gets! I'm going to draw off some more!

TARŌKAJA   You'll be doing the right thing there!

TARŌKAJA   'Za zan za
& JIRŌ   Go the pines beside the sea-side
za zan za....'

(The Master, no longer 'invisible', goes to the first pine.)

MASTER   Well, I've finished my business here, and now I
must be getting along home. This time, I'll bet
those two rascally servants can hardly wait to see
me! *(reaches stage)* Ho ho! I've travelled so fast, I'm home
already! What's all that din? What! Those two fellows are
roaring drunk again! Oh! that pair of crooks! What am
I going to do with them?! Wait a minute! I know what I'll
do!

*(He stands behind Tarōkaja and Jirōkaja, too busy at their revels to
notice him)*

JIRŌKAJA   Oh! Things get jollier and jollier all the time!

TARŌKAJA   Right as always!

JIRŌKAJA   Come to think of it, the Master, thinking he has tied us up good and tight, will be on his way home just about now, taking it nice and easy, without a care in the world!

TARŌKAJA   You're right!   He'll be ambling along nice and easy without a care in the world!

JIRŌKAJA   Fine!   It seems like a good time to give you another drink!

TARŌKAJA   You want to stand me another?

JIRŌKAJA   Sure, old friend!   *(As he looks down at the filled lid, the Master bends forward)*
What!   What's that!?!

TARŌKAJA   What's the matter?

JIRŌKAJA   Take a look at this saké bowl!

TARŌKAJA   Why?   What's in the saké bowl?

JIRŌKAJA   Look for yourself, I tell you!

TARŌKAJA   Right!   Well now, let's see!   What's in the saké bowl? *(looks)*   What!   What on earth sort of thing is that!

JIRŌKAJA   Listen!   Isn't that the image of the Master?

TARŌKAJA   And that's what it is for sure; it's the image of the Master!

JIRŌKAJA   But how come he's reflected in this bowl?

TARŌKAJA   Yes indeed!   How come he's reflected in this bowl?

JIRŌKAJA   I have it!   If you want my opinion, it's because the Master is such a mean old skinflint that although he tied us up, he's afraid we'll get at his saké all the same, and his mind's so uneasy, his obsessed spirit comes like a reflection in the bowl.

TARŌKAJA   I believe you've guessed right!   That's what it is for sure!

JIRŌKAJA   Which reminds me!   I know a great song; when I sing it, you take it up and sing after me!

TARŌKAJA   Right!

JIRŌKAJA   Above one moon

TARŌKAJA   But its reflections

JIRŌKAJA   Here are two or three

TARŌKAJA   Returning waves rise in the nighttime...
& JIRŌ   Bowl with now aboard
The Master hardly seen as Master
By his own two men!   Yo Ho![3]

MASTER   (threatens with closed fan)
What!   You dare talk about me like that!

JIRŌKAJA   Oh me!   Oh my!   It's him!   There'll be the devil to pay!   Quick!   Let's get out of here!

TARŌKAJA   Right!   (they run away to corner)

MASTER   Oh, you pair of scoundrels!   (To Tarōkaja) Hey, you there!   You've had the impudence to go stealing my saké again and drinking it!

TARŌKAJA   Oh no, Sir!   I would never do a thing like that!   It was Jirōkaja!

MASTER   What!   You put the blame on Jirōkaja!   But you are just as bad!   What am I going to do with you?

TARŌKAJA   What are you doing, Sir? Oh, spare me, Sir!   (runs away from threatening Master)   Oh, spare me, Sir!   I

[3]This is a pastiche on poetry from the noh Matsukaze, where two women are dipping brine to make salt (Keene 1970: 25).

didn't mean to do it, Sir!   Forgive me, Sir!   Please, forgive me!   *(exits running down the bridge)*

MASTER   Oh, that rapscallion!   Stop him someone! *(takes a few steps in pursuit)* But Jirokaja!   Where's he gone to?   Now I wonder where he is!   *(turns)*   Hey, you there!   You've had the impudence to go stealing my saké and drinking it!

JIRŌKAJA   Oh no, Sir!   Why would I do that?   It wasn't me at all, Sir!   It was Tarōkaja!

MASTER   What!   And you put all the blame on Tarōkaja.   But you are just as bad!   You're going to get a good thrashing!

JIRŌKAJA   What!   Me!   Innocent as I am!   A thrashing!

MASTER   Precisely!

JIRŌKAJA   If you come after me, I'll really show you how I ward off a night attack!

MASTER   Ward off a night attack!

JIRŌKAJA   Let me up and at 'im!
                (goes after Master, brandishing stick)

MASTER   What are you doing?

JIRŌKAJA   I'll get him!

MASTER   Hey, stop it!   What do you think you're doing!?
                (Master retreats a little)

JIRŌKAJA   Take that!   And now take that!   And that!   And that!
                (pursues Master threateningly)

MASTER   Oh, spare me!   Let me alone!   Oh, please!
                (Jirōkaja runs the Master off the stage)

SEMI

蟬

translated by Carolyn Haynes

CHARACTERS

Shite: Ghost of a Cicada

Waki: Traveling priest

Ai: Local man

SETTING: The village of Agematsu in Shinano Province.

AUTHOR: Unknown

CATEGORIES: This play is categorized variously as a *maikyōgen* (dance kyōgen), *nōgakari kyōgen* (noh-like kyōgen) or a *shukke kyōgen* (priest kyōgen).

188

PERFORMANCE PRACTICES: Performed only by the Izumi
               school.

TEXT: Translation   based on the Izumi text found in No-
               nomura & Andō 1974: 243. Performance notes, available
               only for the final dance, are also of the Izumi tradition, and
               are taken from Nonomura 1935: 23-24.

SOURCES: Parody of typical warrior noh.

189

SEMI (The Cicada)

Translated by Carolyn Haynes

A PLAY IN ONE ACT

(The waki enters wearing a travel cloak over a plain kimono with trousers wrapped and tucked into gaiters. He has on a monk's headdress and carries a rosary.)

shidai WAKI	*(stops at shite spot, faces back)* I wander about, I know not where, I wander about, I know not where, whatever will become of me?
WAKI	*(faces front)* I'm a wandering monk. I've never been to Zenkoji[1] in Shinano Province, so I've made up my mind to go there now. *(greeting pattern)*
michiyuki	In Shinano famous bridges hang between high peaks. Famous, too, the noodles which hang[2] in disarray at Sarashina, where the moon lingers over Mount Asama. *(slowly goes forward few steps)* Near or far, I never know where I'll lodge.[3] *(returns to shite spot)* But here I am at the village of Agematsu.

---

[1]An important temple in present-day Nagano City.

[2]A pun on *soba*, "peaks/ buckwheat noodles;" the latter are a specialty of Sarashina, mentioned below. They are hung to dry.

[3]"Near or far" (*ochikochi*) is probably a reference to a famous poem by Ariwara Narihira (825-80), from the *Tales of Ise*, episode 8; it also appears in the *Shinkokinshū* as poem 903. This poem is alluded to in *Kakitsubata*. The first line of the *michiyuki* is also the same as the first line of the poem: *Shinano naru/Asama no take ni/tatsu keburi/ochikochibito no/mi ya wa togamenu:* Can there be any, near or far,/who fail to marvel at the sight/of the smoke which rises/from Asama peak in Shinano?

I've come so fast, here I am already at Agematsu. Here's a nice pine tree--a fine-looking, lush old tree--
(looks toward center front)
I think I'll rest under it for a while. *(advances to center front)*[4]
But what's this? There's a poem slip hung on it for some reason.
"Dewdrops on a cicada's wing
lie hidden among the trees.
So, too, the tear-drenched sleeves
of my secret, secret longing."[5]
Well! This poem seems to be a special eulogy composed a long time ago for a cicada shell. There must be a story behind this; I think I'll ask someone about it.
(goes to bridgeway and calls out)
Hello, is anyone around?

AI   *(entered earlier, now stands at first pine)*
Who's calling?

WAKI   I'd like to ask about this interesting poem-slip on this pine tree. There must be a story behind it--please tell me what you know.

AI   Well, every summer there are a lot of cicadas on this plain of pine trees, and people gather to listen to them, singing songs and reciting verses and having a good time. Last summer a big cicada lit on this branch, but then birds swooped down and snatched it up. The people thought it quite pitiful, and ever since then they have hung up poem-slips to commemorate it. Even now, some thoughtful person has come and left a poem. You have only a fleeting connection to the cicada, Your Reverence, but do

---

[4]The pine tree is usually not represented on stage.

[5]By Lady Ise, quoted in the *Tale of Genji* "Utsusemi" (Yamagishi 1958: 120). The kyō-gen makes a slight change in the first two lines: *utsusemi no/ ha ni oku tsuyu no,* "dew on the wing of an empty cicada shell," becomes *semi no ha ni/ kakioku tsuyu no,* "dew on a cicada wing," although the implication is still that the shell is empty.

please   say a prayer for it before you   continue on
your way.

WAKI   I'm very grateful to you for telling me all this. I'll go over and
              pray for it before I go on.

AI   If I can be of any further service, don't hesitate to ask.

WAKI   Thank you, I will.

AI   At your service.
              (retires to kyōgen spot, exits through small door when shite en-
              ters)

WAKI   *(goes to center front, kneels)*
              How pitiful, the fleeting existence of a summer ci-
              cada! Its life a dew-drop, it knows neither spring
              nor fall--its world is like a brief dream. "Have faith
              in the Three Treasures, the Three Treasures."[6]
              (goes to waki spot, kneels)

*(The shite enters wearing a travel cloak with the sleeves tacked up, a long
black wig, and a usofuki mask with a puckered mouth.)*

issei   *(goes to shite spot)*
SHITE   "Beneath a tree, the empty shell
              of a cicada who's shed its skin.
              If only I might see once more
              the vanished lady herself!"[7]

WAKI   How strange! Beside my pillow,
              where I've barely laid my head,
              something   appears,   yet   it's   certainly   not   a   person.
              What manner of being are you?

---

[6]*Namu kyara tanno toraya,* a Buddhist invocation. The Three Treasures are the Buddha,
the Law, and the Clergy.

[7]The other poem from the "Utsusemi" chapter of the *Tale of Genji* (Yamagishi 1958:
119). In the original tale, Genji sends this poem to a lady who had defended her virtue by flee-
ing precipitously, leaving a robe behind, when Genji entered her bedroom. Genji compares her
robe, which he has taken as a memento, to the empty shell of a cicada.

SHITE   I am the ghost of the cicada.
           (faces waki)
           In gratitude for your prayers, I have appeared to
           you.

WAKI   So the ghost of the cicada has appeared! I must ex-
           pound the Law for you--it does not differentiate
           between human and creature. We will transform the
           retribution for your evil deeds in life. Tell me in
           detail of your sins--they will dissolve in confession.

SHITE   Yes, I'll tell you about the inescapable torments I
           suffer.
           A flock of crows
           spread their wings at dusk,
           (stamps)

CHORUS   a flock of crows
           spread their wings at dusk,
           and swooped down faster than a kite.
           (goes to center front, jumps)
           One grabbed me, crying,
           "I'll crush you whole!"
           (strikes left hand twice with closed fan)
           He opened his filthy maw
           and crushed me to bits.
           My fellow cicadas
           (opens fan, circles to center back)
           hid among leaves or fled to rotten trees,
           (goes to waki spot, kneels)
           and there wasn't a soul to help me,
           (circles rapidly to shite spot, kneels)
           there wasn't a soul to help me.
           (covers face with fan)

SHITE   And now, to speak of my torments in hell,
           (stands, stamps)

CHORUS   and now, to speak of my torments in hell:
           as was my way in the world of the living,
           *(goes to center front with sweeping movements of
           both arms)*
           I light upon treetops, but now
           (returns to center back)

Their branches turn to swords
and tear through my body.
(jumps)
I fly into the air, but fierce black
mountain spiders have spread their webs
(stamps, goes to corner)
wide across the entire expanse,
and I'm caught in a net of a thousand ropes
(hands to shoulders)
wrapped round and round,
(spins to left two or three times)
round and round and round.
(spins to right 3 times, moving upstage)
And, when the sun goes down,[8]
(sits at shite spot)
I'm dinner for a horned owl
--oh, the misery!
These are the retributions for my sins,
this agony night and noon.
(points to waki, kneels)
But now, o priest, I'll be your disciple.
(bows)
Thus surely I'll be freed from this cycle
and attain buddhahood.
So saying, he takes the tonsure,
(removes wig, drops it at center front)
accepts the Five Precepts,[9]
(goes to waki spot)
and, donning a robe
light as a cicada's wing,[10]
(two stamps, circles right, kneels)
is transformed into Bonze Bug.[11]
(zigzag, closure scoop)

---

[8]*Kurureba*, an extension of the preceding onomatopoeia, *kururi kururi kuru kuru kuru,* "round and round," etc.

[9]The five injunctions followed by lay priests: prohibitions against killing, stealing, adultery, falsehood, and drinking.

[10]*Semi no hagoromo*, literally, "cicada-wing robe," an extremely light-weight summer robe.

[11]A pun on *tsukutsuku bōshi*, a kind of cicada (whose name is said to represent its voice), and *hōshi*, "priest."

HŌSHIGAHAHA

法師が母

translated by Carolyn Haynes

CHARACTERS:

Shite: Husband

Ado: Wife

SETTING: An ordinary household in medieval Japan.

AUTHOR: Attributed to Gen'e, but this ascription is unsubstantiated.

CATEGORY: This play is variously categorized as a *monogurui* (madness) kyōgen, a *nōgakari* (noh-like) kyōgen, or a *onna* (woman) kyōgen.

PERFORMANCE PRACTICES: Performed by all schools: the Ōkura, Izumi, and inactive Sagi.

TEXT: The translation is based on the Ōkura text found in Koyama 1960-61: 2, 213-16. Performance notes are based on lessons with Shigeyama Masayoshi, kyōgen actor of the Ōkura school, in 1985.

SOURCES: The noh *Tango monogurui*.

197

HŌSHIGAHAHA (The Baby's Mother)

Translated by Carolyn Haynes

ACT ONE

(The shite enters, staggering down the bridge, singing. The upper portion of his outer robe is worn very loosely, indicating drunken dishevelment.)

SHITE Zazan-za!
The pines on the beach
Whisper in the wind--
Zazan-za!
(laughs)
Oh, I'm drunk, I'm drunk, I'm **really** drunk! *(at the shite spot)*
Huh, home already.
(goes to bridge, faces curtain and calls)
Hey, where are you? Wife, hey wife--you there?

(The ado enters wearing a kimono and a wrapped-towel headdress used in kyō-gen in place of a wig to indicate female roles)

ADO *(stops at third pine)*
It looks like he's back.
(goes to first pine)
Well, well, you're home, are you?

SHITE What's this, *(mimicking her)* "You're home, are you?"

ADO Yes, that's what I said.

SHITE Where've you been, that I had to shout so loudly?

(During the following dialogue, the shite slowly crosses to left center stage.)

ADO I was having tea at the neighbor's.
(crosses to shite spot)

SHITE *(sneering)* Tea at the neighbor's, is it?

ADO	Yes, that's right.
SHITE	Oh no, you can't fool me! Every time it's the same story-- when I return through the front door, you go out the back; and if I come home through the back, you disappear out the front! I won't take it anymore!
ADO	Oh dear, not again. You've been drinking and now you're talking nonsense. Go on inside and lie down.
SHITE	I don't **want** to lie down. I'm through with you--get out!
ADO	You're being ridiculous! You shouldn't say things like that, even as a joke! Now please, just go inside and rest.
SHITE	Idiot! Your husband divorces you and you still won't leave?
ADO	You mean you're serious?
SHITE	Absolutely.
ADO	Well, if you really mean it, I guess I'll have to go. But usually, when a wife's sent back, her husband gives her something, just a handful of dust.[1] So at least let me have a little trifle, some handful of dust.
SHITE	You want a handful of dust?
ADO	Please.
SHITE	**That's** easy. Here you go-- *(mimes scooping up a handful of dirt and gives it to her)* Now get out of here, fast!
ADO	Oh, you're preposterous![2] That's just a manner of speaking. Give me something personal.
SHITE	Something personal?

---

[1] I.e., a minor token. The husband, however, chooses to take the idiom literally.

[2] *Bukkyō ya, bukkyō ya,* literally, "what madness."

ADO   Yes.

SHITE   Greedy wretch! Well, I guess I shouldn't begrudge you any-
             thing, since I'm getting rid of you. Here, I'll give you this
             robe. *(removes outer robe and hands it to her)*
             Now take it and get out!

ADO   So you really do mean it?

SHITE   Of course I mean it!

ADO   But what about the baby?

SHITE   The baby's none of your business! What are you still doing
             here? Get out right now! Wretch! Shrew! Witch!
             (beats her with his fan)

ADO   Ow! Ouch! Ow! Ouch!

*(Ado flees to the stage attendant spot and sits facing the rear of the stage, "invis-
ible" until she rises later.)*

SHITE   *(at shite spot)*
             Done with that shrew! I feel better already. Think I'll go
             inside and have a good rest. Oh, I'm drunk! I'm really drunk!
             (exits, weaving drunkenly)

ADO   *(stands at the shite spot, with the folded robe poised on her
             head)*
             Oh, this is terrible. I thought it was just his usual drunken-
             ness, but then he really threw me out. I'll be all right, but my
             poor baby! *(weeps)* But there's nothing to be done about it;
             I'll just have to go back to my home village. I'd better get
             going.
             (begins circling the stage)
             I'll bet when Mother and Father hear what's happened they'll
             be really shocked.
             (at center stage)
             Well, here I am already at the highway. My village is so far
             away I ought to rest a bit before going on.
             (sits in back corner)

ACT TWO

issei music (The shite re-enters wearing a broad-sleeved outer robe, with the right sleeve slipped off, and carrying a branch of bamboo grass. Stops at the first pine.)

[issei]
SHITE   "They say that even madness stems[3]
from the workings of saké
on the five organs.
The heart of spring leaps madly,
a bow bent taut to meet the string.
How dear their fragrance, their essence,
the blossoms flowering wildly!
They cannot speak--
yet water ripples, reflected lips do move,
and lo, the blossoms talk."[4]

iroe dance (He enters the stage and performs this brief dance to instrumental accompaniment. The dance is interrupted partway through as he holds his left sleeve to his face in a gesture of weeping and goes toward the waki seat, calling out)

SHITE   Helloo, excuse me--have you seen a woman, no more than twenty years old, pass by this way? You haven't?
(goes to shite spot and calls out)
Helloo, over there, I have something to ask you. Has a woman, just twenty years old, gone by that way? No, no!
(shakes head vigorously)
Not that woman with a maid! Just a woman alone, with her skirts tucked up for walking. She hasn't been this way, either? (continues dancing, stops at center back)
I want to see her again.
My baby's mother.

---

[3]The issei, through "the blossoms talk," is quoted from the noh play *Tango monogurui*, (Yokomichi and Omote 1960-63: 1, 206), altering only a phrase in the second line: "a hindrance in the heart of" becomes "the workings of saké on."

[4]These last three lines, which paraphrase part of a Chinese poem by Sugawara Fumitoki (899-981) in the *Wakan rōeishū*, are also used in the noh plays *Unrin'in* and *Saigyōzakura*.

CHORUS   *(entered earlier and seated themselves at the rear of the stage)*
My distracted heart runs wild.[5]

kakeri dance *(The shite dances to instrumental accompaniment, stopping at back center stage)*

SHITE   My baby's mother is so talented:
(stamps, dances to the following)

CHORUS   *(mimes many of the chorus' words.)*
My baby's mother is so talented:
(stamps)
First of all, in spring she goes to pick fern shoots,
(holds bamboo horizontally, goes forward) then in summer
she plants the rice fields.
(kneels to "plant" the bamboo)
In autumn she toils at the harvest,
(takes corner and circles left)
and come winter she sits at home,
(goes to back stage center)
weaving beside the back window.
Weaving cloth to make our clothes:
(kneels, mimes presenting bolt of cloth)
what does she make with the cloth?
(circles right, folds fingers to count)
Cloaks and trousers and suits for me,
(left hand point, opens and closes fingers of left hand twice)[6]
with padding for warmth,
or unlined for the heat.
(moves forward)
Who will make them for me now?
Oh, how I miss my baby's mother!

[5]There is an untranslatable pun here in the phrase *aitake no midare gokoro*, the sense of which is, "wanting to meet [her] with a distracted heart." But *aitai* ("want to meet") has been changed to *aitake*, a musical term relating to the bamboo instrument *shō*; and the *take* ("bamboo") thus formed serves as a pivot-word leading to the *mi* ("winnow") of *midare* ("distracted"). The sense of the passage is unchanged by these ornamentations, but it warrants mention because it seems to be a conceit borrowed from noh (and possibly other literary forms), as similar puns on *aitai/aitake* occur in the plays *Tokusa* (Sanari 1930-31: 4, 2217) and *Take no yuki* (Sanari 1930-31: 3, 1888).

[6]This movement illustrates the name of one of the robes listed, the *jittoku* (cloak), whose name contains the character for "ten."

(backs up to shite spot, sits, drops bamboo, weeps with both hands to face)

ADO

(stands, the robe on her head, and goes to the waki spot during the following)
The baby's mother, all alone,
stifles her sobs as she makes her way
back to her parents' home.

SHITE

That's the voice I've longed to hear!
(looks up)
Is that you, dear wife?
(gets out fan, kneels)
Forget all this and come on home.
(crosses to ado, pulls at her sleeve, backs up a few steps, drops sleeve)
Leave off your madness, please.
(backs to shite spot, spins around, kneels)

ADO

But I was born with this ugly face.[7]
(shite circles stage, ending with an open towards Ado)
Once we've separated, why should I return?

SHITE

When I called you "ugly,"
(stamps)
when I called you "ugly,"
(stamps)
that was just drunken madness.
(flips the fan open and "drinks")
I **really** think you're pretty.
(beckons twice with fan, crosses to her)

ADO

You really mean it?

SHITE

Of course I do!
(stamps)

CHORUS

"The prettiest girl around.
(stamps)
is the step-daughter of headman Tanaka.

---

[7]This statement makes more sense in the Izumi text (Nonomura & Andō 1974: 449-50), where the husband has earlier stated that he's never liked her looks.

> *(circles stage, ending at shite spot)*
> How I'd like to marry her!
> Namu sambō!"[8]
> *(flaps fan, stamps)*

SHITE   Come on, my sweet, come with me!
           (raises fan)

ADO   All right, dear, I'm coming!

(She crosses in front of him and exits; the shite circles right and follows a short distance behind.)

---

[8]This is presumably a contemporary popular song (*kouta*), although there are no other extant occurrences of it. The final exclamation, which literally means "Praised be the Three Treasures (the Buddha, the Buddhist Law, and the clergy)," lost its religious connotation quite early and appears frequently in kyōgen as an exclamation of surprise or dismay. Here it seems to be used simply for its sound or rhythmic value.

ON THE NATURE OF NOH

Karen Brazell

The nature of noh was shaped in large part by its position in the history of Japanese literature.[1] Japanese drama, of which noh is the first serious example, appeared only after lyric and narrative forms had been highly developed for centuries. Court poetry and popular song, tales, novels and autobiographic works, and religious and scholarly writing were all major forms of discourse before words, music, movement, and visual effects were combined to produce the noh theater in the 14th century. The creators of noh fully exploited their rich heritage, and by doing so produced a theatrical form essentially different from Western drama, which appeared very early in the history of Western literature. One way noh exploited its heritage was by transposing various types of prior discourse into its texts. This transposition, which may also be called intertextuality, has not been fully explored, and one of the aims

[1]Although the author is finally responsible for the contents of this essay, she wishes to thank the various translators who provided ideas and information about the plays they worked on. In addition, the assistant editor, J. Philip Gabriel, offered several important ideas which the author has freely recontextualized in her introduction.

of this essay is to contribute to that exploration by examining the intertextuality of the plays contained in this anthology.[2] Before turning to that main concern, however, it will prove useful to look briefly at two other aspects of noh: the types of the characters presented and noh's rhetorical stances.

Rather than emphasize interaction among characters, noh tends to explore the experience of a single individual (an experience that often extends beyond life in this world) who may or may not be human. Because of this emphasis, plays are sometimes categorized according to the main character's nature. At one extreme are living-being plays, which feature characters who are alive in the play's dramatic present and who exhibit ordinary mental states. These characters are usually human beings like those in *Yoshino Shizuka* and *Bōshibari*, although animals and plants appear as ordinary characters in some kyōgen plays, and the demon in *Oeyama* behaves in many ways like an ordinary being. One step removed from ordinary characters are those whose minds are deranged, usually by the lost of a child or a loved one (*Hōshigahaha*).[3]

At the other extreme are phantoms: deities (in *Unoha* and *Miwa*) or the spirits of plants (*Saigyōzakura* and *Kakitsubata*) and the ghosts of humans (*Unrin'in*, *Genji kuyō*, and *Ikarikazuki*) or occasionally non-humans (*Semi*).[4] In deity/spirit plays some truth or lesson is usually revealed; in ghost plays the individual's past is relived and salvation is sought. There is a connection between the nature of the main character and the way in which time and space are manipulated. Ghost plays usually have more radical disruptions of normal time than any other type of play and consequently are placed at one end of the character axis presented below. Ordinary living-being plays follow normal time the most closely and so are at the other extreme.[5] Between phantoms and living-beings are characters possessed by supernatural beings or by the spirits of other people, living or dead. *Aoi no ue* and *Sotoba Komachi* show people

---

[2]Intertextuality and transposition are both used here in the general sense of "the multiple ways in which any one literary text echoes, or is inseparably linked to other texts, whether by open or covert citations and allusions, or by the assimilation of the formal and substantive features of an earlier text...." (Abrams 1988: 147). For relevant discussions of this concept see Moi 1986 (*Kristeva Reader*), especially p. 111; Bloom 1973; Morson 1981, especially Part 4, "Recontextualizations"; and, for a brief discussion of intertextuality in some Japanese literature, Burch 1979: 37-41.

[3]Noh plays of this type most often portray female characters: *Sakuragawa*, *Sumidagawa*, *Hanagatami*, and *Hanjo* are popular examples.

[4]Noh is less likely than kyōgen to portray the ghosts of noh-human beings, although *Nue*, which features the ghost of a supernatural creature called a *nue*, is a notable exception.

[5]This topic has yet to be fully explored. The most detailed study in English of the dramatic use of time and space in noh is Komparu 1983: 81-95.

possessed by human spirits, and *Miwa* suggests the possession of a person by a deity.

CHARACTER AXIS

Phantom	**Living Being**
ghosts deities/spirits	possessed deranged ordinary

In analyzing a particular play, one should not only be aware of the nature of the character portrayed, but also of the type of rhetoric employed. A rhetorical axis for noh is suggested below:

RHETORICAL AXIS

	Lyric (enacted poetry)	**Expository** (enacted narrative)	**Realistic** (enacted action)
text:	poetry	prose	dialogue
structure:	associative metaphorical	sequential	causal temporal
manner:	abstract stylized	referential	mimetic naturalistic

In lyric theater, or enacted poetry, not only is the text in poetry, but the structure is poetic; it is based on metaphors and associations (both internal to the play and external, reaching out to highly developed poetic and cultural codes, to prior texts, and to the cultural context). Metaphoric structure is essentially spatial; the experience of time is not what is important, rather "the greatest value is gained when the events are considered simultaneously."[6] For example, in *Kakitsubata* the spirit of the iris, the history of the two lovers, and the impetus toward enlightenment are metaphorically fused into one stage figure. Finally, in lyric theater the manner of presentation is abstract and stylized.

---

[6]The quote is from Barry (1970: 123), who is describing how poetry differs from drama. For a related definition of the lyric see Hernadi 1972: 163.

By contrast, realistic drama is enacted action; the text is dialogue, structures are causal and temporal, and the manner of presentation is mimetic and naturalistic. There is, of course, no such thing as a purely lyric or purely realistic play. While a lyric noh play such as *Kakitsubata* is among the world's most lyrical forms of drama, it does contain dialogue, some mimetic movements (although they are highly stylized), and other somewhat "realistic" elements. However, in terms of world drama the noh theater does not reach very far along the axis toward the realistic pole. *Bōshibari* is an example of noh's realistic extreme, yet its high degree of stylization prevents it from approaching the type of realism regularly found in Western drama of the 19th century.

Many noh and kyōgen plays hover around the mid point on our axis, a point that is labelled expository or enacted narrative. The text of expository plays is largely in prose, albeit often a metrical prose, and the structure is basically sequential. In *Ikarikazuki* for example, Noritsune's death is narrated in the *katari* in act one, Niidono (portrayed by the tsure) dies in the *kuse* of act two, and Tomomori's death is depicted by the shite in the final segment of the play. Some stylized dialogue and mimetic actions occur, but the story is more told than shown: the chorus and actors share the lines without regard for a consistent voice (i.e. the chorus may speak for the character and the shite may refer to the character he is presenting in the third person), and the single dancer creates objects and images through referential gestures, presenting more than one character when necessary.[7]

The character and rhetorical axes tend to be parallel; that is, ghost plays are generally the most lyrical, ordinary living-being plays the most realistic. However, there is much variety, and there are many exceptions. Both *Kakitsubata* and *Ikarikazuki* are ghost plays, yet the former is far more lyrical than the latter. The more lyrical plays also tend to be more intertextual than the realistic ones.

Noh in general is one of the most intensely intertextual of all Japanese literary genres.[8] However, the many ways in which a literary text may echo prior texts was acknowledged, valued, and exploited very early in the Japanese literary tradition. Western ideas of originality, plagiarism, and the anxiety of influence were foreign to Japan. Because of this tradition and because noh developed in a society that provided an audience which, although it was expanding and diversifying, still maintained a traditional body of learning and

---

[7]The final part of the play *Tadanori* is a good example of how the shite may switch from character to character (Bethe and Brazell 1982: 2).

[8]Another intensely intertextual genre is *sōga*, a poetic form that probably influenced noh, but which failed to survive as an active genre itself (Brazell 1980).

culture, noh was free to integrate both classical and contemporary materials into its texts.

In using prior texts, the noh playwright often referred not to the original works but to later recontextualizations of them. This is most easily seen in the case of Japanese poetry (waka) which as Noel Burch has pointed out, was "an activity within a context" (1979: 49). Often that context was social: a woman might recite a love poem to her lover, then, when she recorded it in her diary, she might add a headnote explaining the situation (real or imagined) of its composition. Should the poem be selected for an anthology, the editor could put it in a new context: including a love poem in the category of autumn poems for example, and perhaps in the process changing, expanding on, or omitting the original headnote. For a simpler example, a poem about a hut at Mt. Miwa appears without a heading as anonymous poem number 982 in the *Kokinshū*. Minamoto Toshiyori (or Shunrai, fl. early 12th century), however, notes in his poetry treatise *Toshiyori zuinō* that the hut is the dwelling place of the god of Miwa, and this interpretation is the one used by the playwright of *Miwa*.

The *Tales of Ise* is an extreme example of this type of recontextualization. Many poems with identifiable authors are anonymously included in brief "stories" (i.e. new, expanded headnotes) in which the protagonist is often called a "man of old." This "hero" is in turn generally identified as Ariwara no Narihira, who was the author of some of the poems. Hence through the revision and expansion of headnotes an anthology of poetry from various sources became a poetic tale (*uta monogatari*) which was read as a kind of poetic biography.

The majority of the Chinese poems referred to in the noh plays in this volume were anthologized in the *Wakan rōeishū*, compiled around 1013 by the poet and critic Fujiwara Kintō (966-1041) or in the less well known *Hyakuren shōkai*.[9] In neither of these collections are entire Chinese poems given; rather selected lines, usually couplets, are isolated from their original context and presented as "poems." In the case of the *Wakan rōeishū* the Chinese lines are placed side by side with complete Japanese waka.[10] Such couplets are thus freed from their original context to take on a variety of new meanings.

The collection of tales (*setsuwa*), the performance of various types of song and dance, and the pursuit of literary scholarship were activities that

---

[9]The *Wakan rōeishū* has not been translated into English. The text referred to in this anthology is Kawaguchi and Shida 1965. For information about the *Hyakuren shokai* see *Kakei* 1929.

[10]An even closer integration of Chinese and Japanese poetry occurred in the later *wakan renku*, which alternated links in the two languages (Pollack 1986: 140-157).

flourished in the medieval period, and, as all of these endeavors involved the rewriting of classical materials, they served as important mediating texts for noh. For example, the 13th century tale collections *Kojidan* and *Hosshinshū* supplemented the legends about the deity of Miwa and provided material for the play of that name. A Kamakura period song entitled *Genji monogatari hyōbyaku* (A Prayer for the *Tale of Genji*) became the basis for the kuse scene of *Genji kuyō*, while the plot of the play may have been taken from a medieval story (*otogizōshi*) which also incorporated the song. Poetic treatises and handbooks on the *Tales of Ise* provided interpretations that the playwrights of both *Kakitsubata* and *Unrin'in* exploited. Many of these intermediary texts have been ignored by scholars until very recently, and almost none of them have been discussed in English, let alone translated; consequently the role they have played in the creation of noh is just beginning to be understood.

The following discussion of the plays in this anthology not only points out the extent of intertextuality in noh, but attempts to describe some of the many strategies used to incorporate prior texts into noh. There is space here, however, only to suggest the complexity of the subject; each play deserves a complete essay of its own.

From the Age of the Gods

The texts used as sources for both *Unoha* and *Miwa* are myths and legends whose written sources date back to the eighth century, but which were often revised and expanded upon before the plays were composed (probably early 15th century). *Unoha* (Cormorant Plumes) draws on the story of the fourth earthly deity, Hohodemi, who switches his luck-of-the-mountain charm with his brother's luck-of-the-sea charm (a fishhook) which Hohodemi promptly loses in the ocean. In traveling under the sea to recover the hook, he meets and marries the Princess of Ample Gems (Toyotamahime) and receives the Jewels of the Ebb and Flow Tides, which he later uses to control his brother. Back on land, Hohodemi builds the frame of a parturition hut for his pregnant wife and commences to thatch it with cormorant feathers. However, before the thatching is complete, their son is born.

The play emphasizes two objects from this tale, the partially thatched hut and the jewels which control the tides. Both are integrated into the seascape of the play through the images of wind and waves: the thatch is linked to the wind by a play on the word *fuku*, meaning both to blow and to thatch, and the waves of the setting become the tides controlled by the jewels. Both techniques, playing on the polysemic potential of many Japanese words and metaphorically transposing a metaphysical time and place onto the "real" here and now, are typical of noh and will be examined in more detail in the course of this essay.

Act one contains a ritual re-enactment of the thatching of the hut to commemorate the son's birth. The work song accompanying the rebuilding lists numerous items which might, metaphorically at least, be used in thatching, including one which relates the work of thatching to the water imagery: "waves break and scatter white, pearl-like drops of dew, shall we string them together and thatch?" The hut itself is described as the "emblem of the world's immortality and the promise of the gods," and the ritual thatching links the mythic age to the medieval setting of the play.[11]

When the ritual is complete, the waki (a minister of the present emperor) asks the shite (who is costumed as an ordinary woman) whether the jewels of the ebb and flow tides still exist. In affirming that they do, the shite also reveals that she is Toyotamahime (Princess of Ample Gems), the very woman who gave birth in the hut. Her feelings about having her identity discovered are described by quoting a poem which is used in several noh plays:

> Is it a clear gem,
> or what might it be?
> when my love asked
> I should have replied,
> a dewdrop, and perished.

The original context of this poem is episode 6 in the *Tales of Ise* where the hero is running off with his lover.[12] She is the "love" who asked the question about the dew and immediately thereafter was devoured by a demon. The hero in the *Tales of Ise* expresses his grief by wishing that he had not lived long enough to see her die. In the noh play, Toyotamahime wishes that she had disappeared rather than suffer the embarrassment of having her identity revealed. Once she has admitted this, she does disappear, exiting down the bridge to end the first act.

There is probably another echo here that is made explicit nowhere in the play, but which might be picked up by those familiar with the legend: when Toyotamahime gave birth in mythical times, she requested that her husband not look at her. He did, of course, and saw that she had been transformed into a dragon. Ashamed of having her true identity revealed, she disappeared, leaving her husband and son and returning to her ocean home.

[11]Temporal continuity is one of the major features of Shinto thought.

[12]This episode relates Narihira's abduction of Empress Kōshi (Takako), the subject of *Unrin'in* and *Kakitsubata* and is described more fully in the following discussion of *Unrin'in*.

This incorporation of an earlier poem into the *Unoha* text is a good example of a type of intertextuality the Japanese have labelled allusive variation (*honkadori*): the "echoing of the words, sometimes only the situation or conception of a well-known earlier poem in such a way that recognizable elements are incorporated into a new meaning...."[13]

The *Unoha* deity's shame at having her true identity revealed is intensified by comparing it with the original speaker's chagrin at losing his love.

When the shite of *Unoha* re-enters for act two of the play, she is clothed as a deity, and she likens herself to the dragon princess of the *Lotus Sutra* (chapter 12) who "offered a precious gem to Buddha and achieved enlightenment." This allusion and the references that follow it place the jewels of the ebb and flow tides among the gems of Buddhism. As the shite sings and dances about the jewels' power to control the tides, "to make mountains into seas and seas into mountains" (to change the relationship between the brothers), it becomes clear that Toyotamahime wants more: "The jewel of Original Enlightenment. . . is what I desire. Please grant me this!" With this request she disappears into the waves, and the play ends.

The play has taken an old text and rewritten it to present the ritual power that links the Shinto deities of mythic times to the contemporary (medieval) world. In addition, it also places these deities in a new context, that of Buddhism. In Japanese medieval culture Shinto and Buddhist ideas, although often antithetical (at least they appear so in terms of Western logic), were interwoven into a single, multivalent world view and system of practice. What we see in the recontextualization of the myths in this play are Shinto deities both bringing blessings to humans and seeking salvation for themselves, often with human mediation.

Similar themes are presented in an even more complex manner in *Miwa*, a play that interweaves three separate stories: the life of the monk Genpin who lived in the Heian period (the dramatic present of the play), but whose life is most fully described in medieval texts; legends about the deity of Miwa, the shrine near which Genpin lived; and the myth of the Sun Goddess who, in mythical times, hid herself in a rock cave causing the earth to become dark.

The waki plot[14] of the play draws on the first section of the *Gōdanshō*, in which Genpin meets a woman who gives him a robe. On accepting it, he com-

---

[13]Brower and Miner 1961: 506. Related terms include *honsetsu, hikiuta, honmondori*, and *hon'an*. For English explanations see Miner, Odagiri, and Morrell 1985: 277.

[14]The framing plot of a noh play which involves the waki and is always in the dramatic present. It is discussed in more detail below.

poses a poem, which appears in modified form in the play:[15]

> Three circles
> clean and clear
> the Chinese cloak,
> not to be thought of as given,
> nor as taken.

The three circles (*mitsu no wa*) refer to the Miwa Shrine, but also to the three elements of the transaction: the gift and the acts of giving and receiving.

In the play, Genpin's situation is reversed--the waki does not receive a cloak, rather he gives one to a woman (the shite) who arrives daily with offerings for the deity of Miwa. The kyōgen (a local person completing a religious retreat at Miwa) finds the cloak hanging on a cedar tree with the above poem written on it and leads the shite to it. After this discovery, in the beginning of act two, the shite re-appears (dressed as a deity) and presents two stories. The first is about a young woman who, wanting to know her mysterious lover's identification sews a thread to the hem of his garment and, by following it the next morning, discovers that he is the deity of Miwa. The use of needle and thread continue the clothing imagery from the Genpin story.

The second tale, not directly related to the first, is an explanation of the origins of *kagura* (sacred dance). When the Sun Goddess (Amaterasu) retreated to a cave, another goddess performed a dance to lure her out. The shite performs this dance and then depicts the Sun Goddess coming out of the cave. When the sun goddess emerges, the world brightens, day breaks, and the play ends.

In the course of the second act several statements are made about deities: 1) they lead humans to salvation; 2) stories about deities can help people achieve enlightenment, and 3) like humans, deities have desires and seek salvation. Put in other words, the stories presented in the play are redemptive gifts from the Miwa deity, who in turn requests the help of a human, the priest Genpin, to redeem herself. Who is giving what to whom? The gift of a cloak from Genpin in act one has been transposed in act two into the gift of stories

---

[15]The *Gōdanshō* is a collection of tales (*setsuwa*) attributed to Oe Masafusa (1041-1111). The first three lines of the source poem *miwagawa no/ nagisa no kiyoki/karakoromo* (the Miwa River/banks so pure/the Chinese Cloak) have been changed to *mitsu no wa wa/kiyoku kiyoki zo/karagoromo* (as for the three circles/clean and clear/the Chinese Cloak) which emphasizes the number three and the idea of purity.

from (and about) a deity, who wants the gift of salvation.[16] Genpin's "three circles" have taken on new levels of meaning.

Although on the face of it the shite in act two is the deity of Miwa,[17] this play is not classified as a regular, first category, deity play. The reason for this may be that the character should not be considered as the deity itself, but rather a woman possessed by the deity.[18] This observations leads us well beyond the scope of our essay into the larger question of the role shamanism plays in Japanese religion. Suffice it to say for now that *Miwa* may be read as an example of a "possessed" character play, and that it hints at a relationship between the concept of possession and the two-act structure of noh.

Love and Poetry in the Classical Era

The four plays drawing on classical texts (*Unrin'in*, *Kakitsubata*, *Saigyōzakura*, and *Genjikuyō*) are even more lyrical than the two discussed above; not only do all four have poetry as their subject matter, but poetic techniques are their major means of expression. We shall explore very briefly how these plays make elaborate use of allusions, create poetic sequences and catalogues, enact poems, and develop multiplex images. Before turning to these topics, however, we need to look briefly at traditional Japanese poetics, for it too has been integrated into noh, especially in plays drawing on the *Tales of Ise* and the *Tale of Genji*, two classical works which were objects of considerable scholarly interest in the late Heian and the medieval periods.

In *Unrin'in*, for example, the waki is an ardent student of the *Tales of Ise*, and his travel is motivated by a dream in which Narihira and the Empress Kōshi appear in the setting of the Unrin Temple. He travels to that temple where, in a dream vision, he learns a secret or two about the work he loves. The nature of the secret he learns depends on which of the two versions of the

---

[16]From an even broader perspective, the performance is the gift of the actors to the audience, who by attending offer the actors the opportunity to develop their skills and hence to work toward enlightenment, as mastery in any field was thought to lead to universal truth. On this last point see Konishi 1985.

[17]The nature of the deity of Miwa is problematic. In the tale of the woman who follows her lover, the deity is clearly male. In some versions of that story, the lover turns out to be a snake, which leads to the speculation that the "three circles" also refers to a coiled snake. The noh play describes the shite as the deity in female form wearing a man's garb, although current performance practice usually dresses the shite in a female costume.

[18]An even clearer example of this type of possession is evident in the play *Tatsuta*, where the shite in the first act is identified as a *miko* (a Shinto priestess or shaman) and in the second as the deity of Tatsuta.

play one reads.[19] In both versions, however, the secrets refer to section 6 of the *Tales of Ise*, the episode in which Narihira runs off with the Empress Kōshi, who is so naive that she has to ask what dew is (see the poem quoted in the discussion about *Unoha* above), and then she is devoured by a demon.

In the older version of the play, extant in Zeami's holograph, the shite in act two presents the Empress's brother Mototsune, and one of the revealed "secrets" is that the brother was actually the demon--he did not of course "eat" his sister, but re-captured her and returned her to the palace.[20] The more recent version of the play, which probably dates from the latter half of the sixteenth century, has Narihira as the main character in act two and reveals the secret that the names of the places mentioned in describing Musashino Plain where Narihira is supposed to have taken the Empress are actually references to areas inside the palace enclosure. This theory would imply that rather than kidnapping the empress, Narihira simply hid her in the palace. The older version takes this displacement theory one step further by declaring that Musashi equals Kasuga which equals the capital![21]

These secrets, like so many others from the esoteric traditions of medieval Japan, seem uninteresting to the uninitiated. However, the act of transposing one place on top of another (often in the form of layering the sacred on the secular) is common in medieval Japan and is put to good use in noh. For example, two of the exiles on Devil Island in the play *Shunkan* recreate the Kumano landscape in the place of their exile so that they can perform sacred pilgrimages. They are recalled, but the third exile, Shunkan, who refused to participate in the pilgrimages, is not.[22] Another example occurs in the play *Kasuga ryūjin*, where a famous priest is dissuaded from going to India by being assured that Vulture Peak, with all its sacred power, can be found in the landscape of his own Kasuga Shrine.

Another important process in the history of Japanese literature is the compilation of poetry anthologies. This art, a highly sophisticated one in Ja-

[19]The two versions have similar first acts, but differ radically in their second acts. The relationship between these two versions of the texts raise many interesting questions. Most obviously, why was it re-written? One suggestion is that the change was due to the inconsistency created by the shite in the first act suggesting that he is Narihira, only to reappear as Mototsune (Yokomichi & Omote 1960-63: 1, 147). Konishi (1960: 8) briefly discusses the two versions and cites the discrepancies as part of his argument that the study of noh must include plays no longer in the canon. *Unoha* is an example of such a play.

[20]This "secret" is in fact described in what appears to be an interpolation in the text, a holograph by Teika (McCullough, 1968: 73).

[21]For more detailed explanations of this secret see notes 28, 29 and 43 to the translation.

[22]This is not original to the noh play, but is taken from the *Tale of the Heike*.

pan, involves selecting poems and putting them into new temporal, spatial, and associative sequences (Konishi 1958). For example, the love poems in an anthology may be arranged to describe the course of a love affair, from first attraction to nostalgic or bitter remembrance. Noh makes excellent use of this practice of creating poetic sequences to tell a story or make a point. For example, in the first act of *Unrin'in*, a sequence of poems (or allusions to poems) is arranged to create a poetic debate. The subject of contention is whether or not the waki is justified in breaking off a branch of cherry blossoms, and each side selects poems from the past to uphold it's position.[23] The debate draws to its end, in typical noh fashion, with the two speakers sharing lines. Here they divide a paraphrase of a couplet from the *Wakan rōeishū*: "Who has said blossoms are mute? On the ripples of a wave the reflections of the blossoms move their lips."[24] The play concludes that, although when reflected in the water the cherry blossoms appear to move their lips, the flowers can in fact say nothing, so the poet must speak for them, affirming their beauty and their value. Another paraphrase of these lines ends a debate in *Saigyōzakura*, where the spirit of the cherry blossom must speak out to remind the poet Saigyō of the true meaning and value of the blossoms.

The older version of act two of *Unrin'in* is a complex sequencing of quotes from episodes 12, 6, 65, 123, and 9 of the *Tales of Ise* (plus a few other sources) to depict the love of Narihira and the Empress. The passage is so full of allusions that it makes little sense to readers not thoroughly familiar with the source text, which could be a reason the act was rewritten. However, the unexpected shift in meaning that occurs when part of an early poem is recontextualized is one source of the pleasure of the text. For example, the famous capital bird, which Narihira encounters both here and in *Kakitsubata*, is not asked whether the poet's love is still alive, but rather, "Is Musashi Plain truly in the East? or is it perhaps the capital?"--a question relating to the secret being revealed. Then a field guard at Kasuga is summoned forth, not to go to see when the young herbs will be ready to pluck, as in the original *Kokinshū* poem, but again to verify the geography: "above is Mt. Mikasa, and in the foothills Kasuga Plain."[25]

A debate and the depiction of a love affair are only two of the many ways in which noh uses sequences of poetic allusions. Sometimes a theme or image

---

[23]Very often in the first act of a ghost play, the shite tests the waki before revealing his true identity. Here, in *Unrin'in*, the test is the waki's feelings toward the beauty of the blossoms. In *Ikarikazuki* the shite tests the waki's resolve to be a pure priest by ascertaining whether or not he has anything to do with money.

[24]Poem 117 by Sugawara Fumitoki.

[25]Both poems appear in the *rongi*, the last segment of the play.

is developed through a poetic list, as in *Sakuragawa* (Cherry Blossom River), where the blossoms symbolize both a lost son and the transient nature of life. The highlight of the play is a catalogue of references to blossoms. In *Sekidera Komachi* (Komachi at Sekidera), the poet Ono no Komachi's life is depicted through a sequence of allusions to her poems. However, poetry can be incorporated into noh in even more dramatic ways, as the play *Kakitsubata* illustrates. The story related in this play is the same love affair between Ariwara and the Empress (here referred to as Empress Takako[26]) that informs *Unrin'in*. However, it is presented quite differently.

Kakitsubata creates a "central image," an image whose meanings expand and diversify as the play proceeds.[27] Here the image is that of the kakitsubata, a type of iris which Narihira is supposed to have seen growing at Eight Bridges in Mikawa.[28] Someone in the group of travellers suggested that they each compose a poem on the topic of "the spirit of travel," beginning each line with a syllable from the word kakitsubata. Narihira's contribution is the key poem in this play:

karakoromo	Rare robe of Cathay--
kitsutsu narenishi	its hem from long wearing worn
tsuma shi areba	once by my wife when we were close
harubaru kinureu	how far, far from her
tabi o shi zo omou	I've wandered.

Phrases from this poem, quoted in its entirety in the first dialogue between the waki and shite, reappear throughout the play, and with each recurrence the meanings multiply. The "rare robe of Cathay" becomes the robe (representing the empress) that the shite dons for the second half of the play along with a court hat (representing Narihira and his career). Thus clad, the shite, who claims to be the spirit of the kakitsubata, also depicts both partners in the love affair. The concrete connection between these significations is that

---

[26]Takako is the Japanese reading of the Chinese characters for Kōshi, the sinified reading. She is also called the Empress of the Second Ward (Nijō).

[27]How such images are developed in other plays including *Izutsu*, which is also about Narihira, is discussed in Brazell 1981.

[28]From episode 9 in the *Tales of Ise*. This poem is also used in *Unrin'in*.

the iris serves as a memento (*katami*) of Narihira. Furthermore, the text reveals that Narihira is both the Bodhisattva of Song and Dance and the God of Conjugal Love, ideas taken from *Tales of Ise* scholarship.

The same body of *Ise* scholarship claims that the setting for this poem, Eight Bridges, represents eight of Ariwara's lovers ("his thoughts divided as this spider-legged bridge"), some of whom are enumerated in a sequence of poetic allusions in the *kuse* section of the play. And, through allusions to several other poems, the kakitsubata's color, *murasaki* (purple), is shown to signify love or passion which, in the Buddhist scheme of things, deludes those involved and prevents their enlightenment. However, the dark purple of the kakitsubata as memento is discarded, like the Cathay robe to which it is related, "for sleeves of dazzling white" as dawn breaks revealing "glimmering clouds of pale purple," a reference to the clouds on which Amida Buddha descends to welcome the faithful to his paradise and a shade that is now applied to the kakitsubata, whose "heart of enlightenment unfurls," as "trees, grasses and all the earth acquire with her enlightenment's fruit," and the play ends.

This brief analysis is much too cryptic to do justice to the play and it's central image; all it is meant to do is to express the complexity, the profundity, of the play and to illustrate the poetic nature of the play's structure. The plot is insignificant and the story unimportant in relationship to the poetic image which expresses the play's theme. This play is an eloquent illustration of Barry's definition of lyric structure quoted above: "the greatest value is gained when the events are considered simultaneously."

Another way to present poems on the noh stage is to enact their content and/or their context, a technique employed in *Saigyōzakura*.[29] In this play, generally considered to be by Zeami,[30] the poet, Saigyō (1118-1190), portrayed by the waki, is at his hermitage in Saga where there is an old cherry tree famous for its blossoms. When his meditation on Buddhism and the nature of life is disrupted by a crowd wishing to view the blossoms, the waki composes this poem:

> To see the flowers
> is the reason I am told
> why people flock here.
> Hardly fitting, but the fault
> lies with the wretched cherry tree.

---

[29]The enactment of the content of a poem in another of Zeami's plays, *Atsumori*, is discussed in Brazell 1982-83.

[30]The best discussion in English of the authorship of plays linked to Zeami is Hare 1986: 41-47.

This poem actually is by Saigyō and is anthologized both in his private anthology, the *Sankashū*, and in the 14th imperial anthology, the *Gyokuyōshū*. In both places it has the headnote, "Written when I was hoping to remain quiet, and a crowd of people came to view the cherries." What act one of the play does then is to quite straightforwardly enact the creation of the poem in a context similar to the one originally ascribed to it.

However, Zeami only begins there; the enactment of the poem's creation is the waki plot, but the shite's story is yet to come. No sooner has the waki Saigyō recited this poem than the crowd disappears through the side door, and the cloth surrounding the prop is dropped to reveal an old man, who takes issue with Saigyō for blaming the flowering Cherry:

> If I may be so bold as to say so, such an attitude is open to question. The world of sorrows and the hill retreat are in a man's own heart, and the flowering of unfeeling trees and grasses has nothing to do with your human vale of tears. It is therefore without blame.

Because the blossoms cannot speak for themselves, as we saw above in our discussion of *Unrin'in*, the spirit of the blossoms, temporarily incarnated as an old man, speaks for them. To put it another way, the inspiration for much of Saigyō's poetry (i.e. the cherry blossoms) chides him for the view expressed in his poem and then continues in defense of blossoms. The heart of the play (the *kuse*) is a list of places famous for their cherry blossoms. It is a poetic map, or one might say mandala, of the capital.[31] There are some allusions to old poems in this segment, but the text appears to be largely Zeami's own poetry, in which he draws on everything from ancient legends, including one about the Buddha on Vulture Peak, to contemporary objects, such as the blossoms at the Konoe palace which were greatly admired by the Shogun Yoshimitsu.

Another type of poetic catalogue occurs in *Genji kuyō* (A Memorial Service for Genji), where the titles of 26 chapters of the book are woven into the text of the play.[32] The shite (the ghost of the author Murasaki Shikibu) wants prayers said for the *Tale of Genji*, her famous novel, and in the *kuse* segment the chapter titles are linked together to create a sermon on Buddhism, so that the book becomes, in effect, an extended prayer for itself. For example, the titles of chapters three and four are linked in this passage: "De-

---

[31]Compare the sōga "Blossoms" translated in Brazell 1980 and the catalogue of blossoms in *Sakuragawa* (Huey 1983).

[32]Two of the titles are repeated for a total of 28, the number of chapters in the *Lotus Sutra*.

spise this world, empty as a *cicada's shell*, and understand that life is but dew on an *evening face*" (name of a plant as well as a chapter title). This is similar to the technique described in *Saigyōzakura*, where a text becomes the action of the play.

Chapter titles in the *Tale of Genji* are often lines from poems that express a major theme or highlight an important scene in the chapter involved. These titles, actually poetic phrases, were in turn often incorporated into later poetry, and they are used extensively in at least two other noh plays based on the *Tale of Genji*, *Suma Genji*, and *Go*. The titles were also woven into a Kamakura period song entitled *Genji monogatari hyōbyaku* (A Prayer for the *Tale of Genji*) which was then incorporated into a story *Genji kuyō sōshi* (A Tale of the Memorial for *Genji*) sometime in the fourteenth century. The story tells of a nun who visits priest Seikaku at the Agui Temple and asks him to perform a service commemorating her transcription of the *Lotus Sutra* on a copy of the *Tale of Genji*. She has chosen to do this because she found herself attached to *Genji* even after having taken religious vows. The priest offers a prayer (the text of the prior song) and ends with an entreaty to "save Murasaki from the sufferings of transmigration." The framework of the play appears to come from this story, and the *kuse* is an abridgement of that prayer, the original *Genji monogatari hyōbyaku*.[33]

The noh, true to its nature, borrows freely from this material, but also complicates the original context. In the play it is Murasaki Shikibu who asks the priest to hold a memorial service at Ishiyama Temple (where Murasaki is said to have begun writing her masterpiece) for Genji (the term appears to include both the work and the character by that name) and for its creator, Murasaki herself: "Hail Amida Buddha of the West. From the sin of foolish words and fancy phrases absolve Lady Murasaki and grant her salvation in the world to come." Moreover, the text goes on to reveal that Murasaki is the "incarnation of Ishiyama's Kannon, who appeared briefly in this mortal world to set down in writing the *Tale of Genji*...a parable to tell mankind that the world is but a dream." Appearances are misleading. Lady Murasaki is Kannon, and the *Tale of Genji*, far from being just a lot of "foolish words and fancy phrases" is a parable to enlighten mankind. The priest, who is praying for Murasaki and Genji, can himself be enlightened by the artist and her creation as, of course, can the audience who learns from the play. Once again, the giver, the receiver, and the gift (the artist, the audience, and the art) have be-

---

[33]It is possible, though less likely, that the story is based on the noh play. A summary of the story (*sōshi*) and the complete text of the song *hyōbyaku* are given in Ito, 1986: 434-437. To complicate matters even further it is possible that there was a kusemai dance that used this text (Konishi 1972: 3). The textual history of this and other *Genji* plays is dealt with at length in Janet Goff's manuscript on the subject.

come inextricably interwoven. The chapter titles have become a prayer for the work; the priest, in praying for the soul of another, is in turn presented with the means to his own enlightenment.

In the broadest sense, this is the theme of all the plays discussed thus far. Deities (in *Unoha* and *Miwa*), artists (Ariwara no Narihira and Murasaki Shikibu), and nature, the inspiration for art (the kakitsubata and the cherry) are all shown to be both the givers and the receivers of enlightenment. The gift of enlightenment is embodied in the art, which in turn often embodies the artist. By presenting this complex, intangible unity, the noh attempts to transcend this world's boundaries. A multiplex vision is created, yet each new level of insight both deconstructs and reinterprets the former perspectives. Dream and reality become so entwined that their essential oneness (or should one say their essential emptiness?) is affirmed. The dream (stage reality) disappears as the shite leaves the stage, and the waki (with the audience) is left with the memory of a vision. The art of interweaving texts in new and ever changing contexts expresses the basic message and the basic aesthetic of phantom noh: nothing is ever what it seems.

Medieval Warriors, Women and Demons

The characters portrayed in *Ikarikazuki* are also phantoms, but the play's rhetoric is more expository than lyric. The play narrates the deaths of three people in the battle of Dannoura, the decisive defeat of the Heike clan in 1185, drawing on the account in the *Tale of the Heike*.[34] In the tale Lady Niidono plunges into the ocean with the young emperor Antoku and dies. Thereafter, Ladies Kenreimon'in and Dainagon attempt to drown themselves, but are pulled from the water by the Genji. Numerous warriors also jump overboard: two of them (Noritsune's father and uncle) shoulder anchors. Noritsune jumps in with an enemy soldier under each arm, and Tomomori puts on a double suit of armor and drowns hand in hand with his foster brother.

From this jumble of suicides, the playwright has chosen to focus on three, rearranging the order of their occurrence and, in one important instance, the details of the death. The initial encounter between the waki (a traveling priest) and the shite (a fisherman) juxtaposes the sacred and the secular, develops the theme of Buddhist salvation, and introduces images of boats and the sea. When the waki asks the shite for tales about the ancient battles, the shite begins, for no apparent reason, with the death of Noritsune, which is told in a *katari* (narrative) segment with the shite costumed as an old fisherman and

---

[34]The passage the play is based on is translated in McCullough 1988: 376-381.

seated on a stool to give the recitation. At the end of the segment, he announces that he is "the ghost of those who sank into the waves," requests prayers, and disappears.[35]

In act two the ghosts of Ladies' Niidono and Dainagon (tsure) and Taira Tomomori (shite) appear in a boat prop. Niidono and the chorus describe, in a *kuse* segment, how she went to her death with the young emperor in her arms, and then the two tsure depart the stage by the side door. Once they are gone, the shite comes out of the prop and, in strong movements and martial rhythms, portrays the battle, manipulating a halberd as he dances, and compares the war to the battles of the asura, those titanic beings who are in constant combat. Finally, the text tells how Tomomori dons two suits of armor, drapes an anchor on top of his helmet, and drowns. (The stage figure dances with a fan and mimes the crucial actions.) The playwright has taken liberties with his source here; no other text has been found in which Tomomori drowns with an anchor. In the *Tale of the Heike* it is Noritsune's father and uncle, and in one version of *Genpei seisuiki* it is Noritsune. The image is, however, a striking one and makes a dramatic ending to the play.[36]

Ikarikazuki is clearly a play about warriors and war; however, unlike most second-category warrior plays, it does not explore the emotions of a single character, rather it narrates a battle scene more generally, describing the deaths of three people. Each of the characters depicted has his or her own integrity; their stories are told separately and sequentially. This method of presentation contrasts sharply with the lyrical mode used in a play like *Kakitsubata*, where the various characters presented by the shite meld into one complex figure. However, the presentation in *Ikarikazuki* is not particularly realistic, even for noh. The logical causal structure of the *Tale of the Heike*, where the death of the emperor is the reason for Noritsune and the others to commit suicide, is undercut by depicting Noritsune's death first. Also the juxtaposition of the earthly battles with metaphysical asura combat, a juxtaposition that emphasizes the transience of this life and the hellish nature of war, is clearly an example of metaphoric structuring. In short, *Ikarikazuki* is a phantom play with an expository style; it lies somewhere between the lyrical plays discussed above and the more realistic plays we now turn to.

---

[35]The identity of the shite in act one is far from clear. Here the plural (*hitobito no yūrei*) is used with unclear referents. The text of the interlude given in Sanari 1930-31: 257 identifies the fisherman as Tomomori; however, because the shite describes the death of Noritsune, sometimes commentators identify him with that warrior (Nogami 1971: 457). The role of the shite in the play *Yashima* is comparably vague (translated in Tyler 1978a).

[36]When this story is transposed into a kabuki play the anchor appears as an enormous stage prop.

The play *Yoshino Shizuka* (Shizuka at Yoshino) is an interesting combination of lyric, expository, and realistic elements. Yoshitsune, the Genji victor at Dannoura, is the subject of numerous accounts and legends, beginning with the *Tale of the Heike* and culminating in an anonymous 15th century tale entitled *Gikeiki* (The Record of Yoshitsune).[37] Yoritomo, the founder of the Kamakura shogunate and Yoshitsune's half-brother, turns against Yoshitsune, hunts him down, and finally has him killed. At one point in his wanderings Yoshitsune takes refuge in the Yoshino mountains with his mistress Shizuka and a faithful retainer Satō Tadanobu. According to the *Gikeiki*, Yoshitsune sends Shizuka back to the capital with an escort which promptly deserts her. All alone she happens upon a Yoshino temple where a festival is in process, and she is persuaded to offer a song to the deity. Consequently, she is recognized by the monks and forced to reveal Yoshitsune's whereabouts. The monks attack Yoshitsune, who flees, leaving Tadanobu with some retainers in the mountains to prevent pursuit. He succeeds, though all his men are killed in the process.

The plot of the play is very different. The original form of act one is unknown, but in the 18th century Kita text translated here, Tadanobu (the waki) and Shizuka (the shite) meet in Yoshino, discuss Yoshitsune, and plan how they might help him. They decide that Tadanobu is to pretend to be a pilgrim, attend a meeting of the soldier-monks who want to capture Yoshitsune, and try to persuade them that the two brothers are reconciled so that there is no need to rush out in pursuit, while Shizuka is to offer a sacred dance to the deity of the shrine. Act one ends as the two characters depart to prepare for their roles. The meeting of Tadanobu and the monks (two kyōgen players) is depicted in the Interlude.

Only act two of this play is commonly performed today, and it depicts Shizuka dancing at a Yoshino shrine to distract the enemy and delay their pursuit of Yoshitsune.[38] Shizuka's performance for the soldier-monks has two parts: the first, presented in the *kuse* scene, relates the source of enmity between Yoshitsune and Kagetoki. It explains that Kagetoki slandered Yoshitsune to his brother because Yoshitsune had accused Kagetoki of being a coward in what is known as the "reverse oar controversy."[39]

The *kuse* is followed by a dance to instrumental music, framed by a poem with an interesting history. It is recorded as a love poem in the *Tales of Ise*,

---

[37]Translated by H. McCullough simply as *Yoshitsune* (1966).

[38]Creating a performance within the performance is a technique used in many noh plays. *Atsumori* and *Jinen koji* are two examples.

[39]Taken from the *Tale of the Heike* chapter 11 (McCullough 1988 358-360).

episode 32, and literally translated reads:

inishie no	an old time
shizu no odamaki	bobbin for shizu cloth
kurikaeshi	rewind it,
mukashi o ima ni	make past into present
nasu yoshi mo gana	how I wish I could

The poet is longing for the time when the lovers were as close as threads on a bobbin.

According to the *Gikeiki*, when Shizuka was forced to dance for Yoritomo at Tsurugaoka Shrine in Kamakura, an event that occurred after Tadanobu's death, she chose to sing a variation of this poem with the first lines changed to *shizu ya shizu/shizu no odamaki*. The word *shizu*, which signifies a kind of old-fashioned, striped cloth, can also be read to mean "calmly" (*shizuka*), hence: "quietly, serenely like the shizu bobbin." In the new context, the syllables evoke the name of the dancer herself, and having Shizuka as the speaker the sentiment, "I wish there were a way of bringing back the past" implies not only longing for a loved one, but a wish to restore Yoshitsune to power and prestige. His jealous brother Yoritomo did not appreciate the suggestion, "That was a brazen exhibition!"[40] Thus the audience of the noh play might read this poem as seditious; however, the soldier audience within the play, entranced by the beauty of the dance, allows Yoshitsune to escape, and Shizuka returns to the capital, her mind serene (*kokoro shizuka ni*).

Yoshino Shizuka is a living-being play, that is the characters are alive in the dramatic present. Consequently, time is used quite differently than in phantom plays. In many ghost plays, for example, time is reversed--the past is re-created on the stage--for the ghosts of noh wish to re-experience their past lives in order to gain new understanding and to make progress on the path to enlightenment.[41] On the other hand living characters usually remain within the present, and the structures of plays of this type are likely to be temporal and causal. *Yoshino Shizuka* has many lyrical elements; it uses poetry and abstract dance very effectively in Shizuka's performance for the monks. However, in terms of the waki plot that performance functions causally--it prevents the soldiers from pursuing Yoshitsune.

The waki plot, which I have mentioned only in passing above, is the frame of a noh play; it relates what happens to the waki, who is always a living

---

[40]The story is recorded in the *Gikeiki* (Okami 1959: 296-297 or McCullough 1966: 235).

[41]Descriptions of suffering in hell as in *Kinuta* and *Motomezuka* depict the dramatic present, but not life on earth, rather suffering in hell.

character.[42] Because the waki plot always occurs in the dramatic present, it is likely to have more importance in living-being plays than in phantom plays. In many of the latter, the waki is an unidentified man,[43] usually a priest (in *Kakitsubata* and *Ikarikazuki*) or a courtier (*Unoha*), who travels (or is residing in retreat) and encounters an ordinary looking person (the shite). He learns who that person is, settles down for the night (sometimes in prayer), and then witnesses the presentation of the shite's story (most often in the second act after the shite has returned costumed as his or her true self). In this simple plot the waki is an observer: his own story is unknown; his function is basically to elicit and then to witness the shite's story, which may be the re-creation of events from the shite's past life, the enactment of a ritual, or the explanation of a "truth" about religion or literature. In this kind of play the waki may be seen largely as a representative of the audience.

Sometimes the waki is given a personal identity, and the phantom appears because the waki is who he is: in *Genji kuyō* the waki is a priest from Agui Temple where the Genji prayer was written, and in *Unrin'in* the waki is Kinmitsu, a student of the *Tales of Ise*. The waki Genpin in *Miwa* is more involved in the play for he is the author of the poem that presents its theme. However, his role in the performance is still comparatively simple: he introduces himself, talks to the shite, and follows the kyōgen to a hut near a cedar where he witnesses the shite's story. Saigyō, the waki whose poem is enacted in the first part of *Saigyōzakura*, has an active role vis a vis the crowd (the kyōgen), yet once the shite begins his presentation, he too is simply the viewer.

The role of Tadanobu, the waki in *Yoshino Shizuka*, is only slightly more impotant: he describes his situation, meets Shizuka, schemes with her, attempts to carry out his part of the scheme, encourages the shite to play her role, and only then recedes to the position of witness--here as part of the stage audience for the performance within the performance, Shizuka's dance. Shizuka is of course the main stage figure, and it is her art--the beauty of her dance--which is the major focus of the play. However, the verbal part of the shite's story is not a revelation about the character Shizuka, but an explanation of why Yoritomo and Yoshitsune have become enemies; even this is an element of the waki plot, which is clearly more important here than in any of the other plays discussed above.

---

[42]Some plays do not return to a mention of the waki at the end, but the stage figure is almost always present to remind the audience of his "plot."

[43]The waki role is always played unmasked and as noh actors were traditionally all male, and waki actors are still, the character the waki portrays is always male. Secondary female figures are played by tsure.

The waki plot is even more important in the last noh play in our anthology, *Ōeyama*. This play might be labelled a living-being play, if one believes, as medieval people did, that demons are living beings. The demon is Shuten Dōji, literally "Wine-drinking Lad," a legendary demon chieftain whose benign aspect is that of a youth, and who is said to abduct women from the capital. A late fourteenth-century picture scroll entitled *Ōeyama ekotoba* contains an early written version of the story which is latter retold in medieval tales (*otogizōshi*) and other genres. The man who quells this demon is Minamoto no Yorimitsu (948-1021), whose name is also pronounced Raikō. Yorimitsu, a warrior aristocrat, poet, and provincial governor, was famed as an archer, and his name gradually became associated with various martial tales and theatrical pieces.[44]

In the play *Ōeyama*, Yorimitsu (the waki) and five or six warriors (wakizure),[45] disguised as mountain ascetics, are off to Ōe Mountain with orders to subdue the demon who dwells there. When they arrive, they send a servant (kyōgen) to request lodging. The servant meets a woman (another kyōgen) who has been abducted by the demon, and asks her to secure lodgings for them. The demon (the shite) appears in his benign aspect as a temple youth (dōji). The travellers get the "youth" to describe his personal history, and then they all drink together until, quite drunk, the demon retires. The interlude is a scene between the servant and the woman during which he persuades her to become his wife. In act two, the actors remove their monkish disguises, go into the bedroom, and discover that the "youth" has changed into a demon. What actually happens on stage is that the attendants bring in a tatami dais with a covered frame prop on it, and they remove the covering to reveal the demon at the appropriate moment. A fight ensues and the demon is killed.

As a stage figure Yorimitsu is clearly upstaged by the demon, yet the character Yorimitsu is central to the action of the play. The waki is not the observer of the demon, but its slayer. The waki plot is clearly more important than the shite story, which in this case is simply a brief recounting of the demon's past life in a question-and-answer passage (*mondō*) early in the play.

The kyōgen also play a more important role in *Ōeyama* than in the other plays we have discussed. In *Unoha*, *Unrin'in*, and *Ikarikazuki* the kyōgen appear in the interlude to retell or comment on the shite's story. In *Miwa* the kyōgen, a pilgrim in retreat at Miwa, discovers Genpin's cloak and informs

---

[44]He also appears in the noh plays *Tsuchigumo* and *Rashōmon*. The bunraku and kabuki plays in which he appears are called Raikōmono.

[45]The text names six; how many actually appear on stage can vary from performance to performance.

Genpin of it whereabouts, whereas in *Yoshino Shizuka*, the kyōgen represent the monk-warriors wishing to pursue Yoshitsune. The waki interacts with them in the interlude, and although they have actually left the stage, they are the presumed audience of the shite's presentation in act two. In *Ōeyama*, however, not only do the kyōgen participate in the waki plot--they get the waki and wakizure admitted to the demon's hideaway and provide them with a key to the bedroom--but they also have their own subplot, their own story: the male servant courts the woman and convinces her to marry him.

There are not many noh plays in which the kyōgen create their own subplots.[46] Parallel comic-servant and serious-master plots only appeared regularly in Japanese drama with the development of the puppet and kabuki theaters (17th and 18th centuries).[47] In the noh theatre, lowly, comic characters appeared in their own plays: the kyōgen plays performed between the noh pieces.

Follies and Foibles (Kyōgen Plays)

The three kyōgen plays anthologized here do not begin to represent the variety of the 260 plays performed in the current repertories, but they do present two important types of kyōgen--those that parody noh directly and those that present (and are commentaries on) contemporary medieval life.[48] Even the most domestic kyōgen, however, may draw on noh in several ways.

The kyōgen play *Bōshibari* is about living beings, ordinary servants and a master, and it is as far to the realistic end of the rhetorical axis as plays in the noh theater ever get. The text is entirely in dialogue (no chorus appears), although the actors occasionally speak in unison, and at one point Jirōkaja describes the opening of the door onomatopoeically (*garari garari*) as he mimes the action. The plot is clearly causal (a master ties up his servants to prevent them from drinking his sake, but they figure out how to get at it) and the expe-

---

[46]The kyōgen may be important to the waki subplot, as in *Dōjōji* and *Kurozuka*, or they may have their own little story as in some variants of *Tama no i, Tomoe, Hashibenkei, Youchi Soga,* and *Arashiyama,* but in the latter case there is no direct relationship between the kyogen story and the noh play characters.

[47]There is some evidence that kyōgen played a more humorous role in early noh plays. A remnant of this might be the kyōgen's parody of the *shidai* in the play *Ataka* (Yokomichi and Omote 1960-633, 2: 169). Also, Zeami makes it a point to state that the kyogen's function within noh plays is NOT to amuse the audience (Rimer and Yamazaki 1984: 170).

[48]Although kyōgen originated side by side with noh, written texts developed much later, probably because the plays were largely improvised. The earliest extant text, the *Tenshō kyōgenbon* of 1578, gives only summaries of the plots. The earliest full texts are the *Kyōgen rikugi* (c.1624-43) and *Ōkura Toraakirabon,* 1642.

rience in time is crucial (Will they manage to get the sake? Will they get caught?). Although the movements are often mimetic, they are always extremely stylized. The language too is colloquial (at least it was when the play originated), yet it is spoken in a highly stylized manner.

In addition to the plot, there is also a presentational aspect to the play which provides much of the pleasure of the performance but is completely missed in the reading experience. As they drink their sake, the two servants dance and sing to amuse each other--as well as the audience, of course. The dances are kyōgen *komai*, the songs (which vary according to the performance) are often passages from noh plays. Later, a textual and kinetic allusion to the noh play *Matsukaze* helps to highlight a climatic moment in the play. When the master returns home and finds his tied-up servants drunk, he sneaks up behind them. They are first aware of his presence when they look into the sake bowl which is sitting on the floor between them. When they recognize the reflection of their master in the sake, the following dialogue occurs:

JIRŌKAJA	...I know a great song. When I sing it, you take it up and sing after me.
TARŌKAJA	Right!
JIRŌKAJA	"Above one moon
TARŌKAJA	but its reflections here
JIRŌKAJA	are two or three
TOGETHER	returning waves rise in the night--in the **bowl** our **master** rides but is not considered as **master** by his **servants**"

This quote is a passage from the noh play *Matsukaze*, where two young women are at work filling their little cart with sea water to boil down for salt. The four words in boldface type have been changed in the allusion: the last two lines of the noh passage mean "in the **cart** the **moon** rides; not considered sad, [our life] by the sea."[49] In the noh text the women are able to overcome the sadness of their lives of toil by appreciating the beauty of the moon. The kyōgen, realizing that their drunken revels must end with the appearance of the master, nevertheless go on to revile him. The incongruity of the allusion creates the humor in the situation.

---

[49]The Japanese text is *tsuki wa hitotsu, kage wa futatsu mitsu shio no yoru no kuruma (katazuka) o nosete ushi (nushi) to mo owanu shioro (uchino mono) ka na ya.* The words in parentheses indicate the changes made in the kyōgen, which is given in a more literal version here than in the translation of the play.

This type of intertextuality, the humorous use of noh elements in kyōgen, is common and effective, for kyōgen shares the noh audience and can hence assume its knowledge. Nowhere is the relationship more fully exploited, however, than in the plays whose humor comes largely from parodying noh. Two of these are included in our anthology.[50] *Semi* is about the ghost of a cicada. The waki, a lowly travelling monk, sings a travel song, as would the waki in noh, but with a difference:

> In Shinano
> famous bridges hang between high peaks,
> famous too the noodles which hang
> in disarray at Sarashina,
> where the moon lingers over Mount Asama.
> Near or far, I never know where I'll lodge.

Here Sarashina, celebrated in poetry for its beautiful moon, is also connected with noodles, a more mundane specialty of the place. Shinano is described in a poem from the *Tales of Ise* (which is also quoted in the *kuse* segment of *Kakitsubata*):

> From Asama Peak in Shinano
> smoke spirals upward
> Can there be any, near or far,
> who fail to marvel at the sight.

In *Semi* the waki does not marvel from near or far (*ochikochi*), rather he focusses on the more down to earth issue of whether he will be able to find lodgings, near or far.

What the waki does find hanging on a tree is a slip of paper containing a poem from the *Tale of Genji* about a cicada. After a local man tells him how a cicada died in the same spot last summer, the ghost of a cicada appears, quotes another cicada poem from *Genji*, tells of his own death in "battle" with a flock of crows and of his current torments in hell. He prays and is "transformed into a Bonze Bug." The form and general content is familiar from noh, yet the character and tone are not: the warrior of noh has been transformed into a bug! The parody here is not simply textual: the ghost of the cicada is costumed like a typical noh ghost, but with a funny mask. The use of musicians, chorus and dance all mimic noh as well.

Like *Semi*, the play *Hōshigahaha* parodies noh, but in a much gentler fashion. Here we find not a warrior dying in battle and suffering in hell, but a

---

[50]Carolyn Haynes, the translator of these plays, has written a Ph.D. dissertation on plays of this type which contains much fuller analyses of the two plays discussed here (Haynes 1988).

deranged person searching for a loved one. Noh plays of this type most often feature a person, usually a woman, searching for a lost child. In *Hōshigahaha* we have a man who abruptly divorces his wife when he is drunk then repents his action and goes out in search of his child's mother. He enters in act two and sings this passage:

> They say that even madness stems
> from the workings of saké on the five organs
> the heart of spring leaps madly
> a bow bent taut to meet the string.
> How dear their fragrance, their essence,
> the blossoms flowering wildly.
> They cannot speak--
> yet water ripples, reflected lips do move,
> and lo, the blossoms talk.

The last three lines are yet another rendition of the poem that ended the debates between waki and shite in both *Unrin'in* and *Saigyōzakura*. In those plays the lines helped to express the relationships among nature (the inspiration for poetry), poetry, and poets. Here the function of the allusion is quite different: it expresses the deranged state of mind of the shite who knows blossoms to be mute, yet he sees them open their lips and speak.

Hōshigahaha is a remarkable kyōgen. The play as a whole can be seen as a variation of the noh play *Tango monogurui*, from which the above quote comes.[51] The kyōgen play transposes a father-son relationship to a husband-wife story, but in doing so it resorts to none of the burlesque found in the other two plays, rather it is a humorously sympathetic rendition of a very human situation. One of the most touching elements is the lovely list of the wife's talents, presented in the order of the seasons, and mimed in dance by the shite to the song of the chorus. This is clearly a different kind of noh parody. Whereas *Semi* makes fun of specific conventions and motifs of the warrior noh, and does so with an incongruity of form and content which renders the subject rather silly, *Hōshigahaha* makes liberal use of story elements and quoted passages from *Tango monogurui* to tell its own story straightforwardly--a similar story in a humbler context.

These twelve plays reveal but a small part of the richness of noh. They do indicate, however, how noh has selected stories, ideas, and texts from a broad spectrum of sources, adapted these materials to suit its needs, and infused them with the world view and culture of medieval Japan to create a bril-

---

[51]This play is about a father and son. The text is in Yokomichi and Omote 1960-63: 1, 201-210.

liant, new theatrical form. For the noh theater nothing is too humble, neither cicadas nor iris; nothing too grand, not heavenly deities nor literary master- pieces. And the ways in which noh reads its sources (visually and aurally as well as textually) are so sophisticated that they continue to fascinate modern readers, poets and playwrights.

NOTES ON CONTRIBUTORS

MONICA BETHE resides in Kyoto and teaches at Kyoto Women's College and Kansei Gakuin. As a student of noh practice for around 20 years she has studied mask carving, song, dance, the drums and the flute. Her full noh performances include *Tadanori* (shite), *Kiyotsune* (flute) and *Kakitsubata* (hip drum). She also did the choreography and costuming and played the lead in *Crazy Jane*, a noh inspired dance drama by David Crandall. Her publications include collaborative books with Karen Brazell on performance, English commentary and translations for collections of noh costumes and masks, and articles on costuming and noh training.

KAREN BRAZELL is Professor of Japanese Literature and Director of the East Asia Program at Cornell University. Her works on noh include studies of noh performance with Monica Bethe and several articles. She is currently editing an *Anthology of Traditional Japanese Theater* for Stanford University Press and working on a book-length study of noh tentatively entitled *The Ghosts of Warriors on Stage*.

J. PHILIP GABRIEL is currently a graduate student in Japanese literature at Cornell University. He plans to write his dissertation on the work of the modern author Shimao Toshio. A longtime resident of Nagasaki, Gabriel was co-translator of *Testimonies of the Atomic Bomb Survivors*, 1985), the first such book published in English by the City of Nagasaki. He was also a co-founder and associate editor of Nagasaki's English journal, *Harbor Light*. His latest publication is a translation of a short story by Murakami Haruki which appeared in the Spring 1988 issue of *ZYZZYVA*, a San Francisco-based literary journal.

JANET GOFF received a Ph.D. in Japanese langauge and literature at the University of Michigan and taught for three years at Carleton College. She now resides in Tokyo where she studies noh and, in 1986, performed the shite role in the full noh *Hagoromo*. She has published articles and book reviews on noh and is completing a book-length manuscript on the 15 noh plays inspired by the *Tale of Genji*.

CAROLYN HAYNES is Assistant Professor of Japanese at the University of Texas in Austin, having received an M.A. in Theater Arts from the University of Kansas and a Ph.D. in Japanese literature from Cornell University. She has published two articles on kyōgen and is in the process of turning her Ph.D. dissertation on the parody of noh in kyōgen into a book. She has studied both noh and kyōgen performance in Japan.

H. MACK HORTON is a specialist in Japanese medieval literature. His doctoral dissertation for the University of California, Berkeley, is entitled, "Poetry in Motion: The Linked-Verse Master Sōchō and his Journal, *Sōchō shuki*." He is currently preparing a translation of *Sōchō shuki* under a grant from the National Endowment for the Humanities. Horton has also produced a number of articles and translation-adaptations in the field of traditional Japanese architecture.

EARL JACKSON, Jr. has a Ph.D. in Comparative Literature from Princeton University and is now Assistant Professor of East Asian Studies at the University of Minnesota. He wrote a noh play on the death of Hart Crane entitled *Bridges: A Warrior Nō*, and has also written and performed in several works related to noh. The two most recent are: "Dialogue Between No-One," a multi-media performance piece premiered in Minneapolis on May 13, 1988, and "Takasago in Blue," a concert/video series with Okunari Tatsu (poet/trumpet) and Mitsutomi Toshio (flute) on the Minnesota Public Radio and at the University of Minnesota in April 1988. Jackson is completing a manuscript on "Japanese Symbolist Poetry" and a critical anthology of texts on poetic theory from Meiji through Taishō.

EILEEN KATŌ, who is Irish, was educated in Ireland, France and the United States. Her first M.A. was in French literature from Ireland National University and her second was in Japanese literature from Columbia University. She has published translations of three noh plays, and is currently preparing a book of her noh translations. Her interests include modern plays using the noh formula. She has written one entitled *Nefertiti* which is set in Ancient Egypt's Amarna period, and she is presently working on another based on the Gaelic story of "The Old Woman of Beare." Katō has spent about half of the last 30 years in Tokyo and has lived for extended periods in New York, Paris, Peking, and Cairo. She currently resides in Brussels.

JEANNE PAIK KAUFMAN received an M.A. in Japanese Literature from Columbia University and is currently a Ph.D. student in Japanese and Korean Literatures at Cornell University. For her M.A. thesis she analyzed and translated the otogizōshi, "Kachō fūgetsu." She plans to write her Ph.D. dissertation on Korean writers in Japan.

SUSAN BLAKELEY KLEIN is a Ph.D. student in the field of East Asian Literature at Cornell University. Her interests include contemporary art, theater, and performance, as well as traditional Japanese theater. Her Cornell M.A. thesis on the Japanese avant-garde dance movement,

Ankoku Butō, is being published as a monograph in the Cornell East Asia Papers Series. Klein is currently doing research on medieval commentaries and noh plays related to the *Tales of Ise* and is continuing her work on contemporary Japanese dance/theater.

ETSUKO TERASAKI was the first faculty member to teach Japanese literature at Cornell University. She has published a number of translations, reviews, and articles, including the translation of a novel, *The Silver Spoon*, and a study of Bashō's linked verse. Her research on noh began with her Ph.D. thesis at Columbia, which was entitled "A Study of Genzainō." She has also published critical analyses of several plays. Terasaki's present research projects are a book-length study of the plays attributed to Kan'ami and a collection of translations of Motomasa's plays.

GLOSSARY OF JAPANESE NOH TERMS

This glossary contains brief descriptions of the Japanese noh terms used regularly in the translations of the plays. For more technical definitions see the glossaries in Bethe and Brazell 1982, vol. 3, or Hare 1986. The former also contains illustrations of the dance patterns referred to in the stage directions. The term "segment" is a translation of *shōdan* and refers to the smallest named unit of performance. Each segment has a characteristic form of poetry, rhythm, melody, instrumentation and movement. Words in boldface type have their own entries.

ADO. The designation given to the secondary kyōgen actor(s) in either the interludes of noh plays or in kyōgen plays. In a few noh-like kyōgen, such a *Semi*, the secondary actor is labelled **waki**. Compare **omo**.

AGEUTA. A segment of sung, metered poetry beginning in the upper register. One of the most common segments in noh, it may describe travel (*michiyuki*) or serve as the waki's waiting song (*machiutai*) in the beginning of act two. Often follows a **sageuta**.

AI. An abbreviation of *aikyōgen*, the kyōgen actor who appears within a noh play or who has a similar function in a noh-like kyōgen. In the noh plays in this anthology aikyōgen have simply been labelled kyōgen. The interludes of noh plays are also called aikyōgen. See **kyōgen**.

ASHIRAI MUSIC. Simple instrumental music used to accompany some action of the shite or the tsure. It may accompany a quiet entry, movement from the bridge to the stage, or an onstage costume change.

CHŪNOMAI (medium dance). A long instrumental dance performed to moderate tempo, usually in the abbreviated three-section form. It is used in a wide variety of roles in all five categories of plays and is often considered the standard dance.

CHŪNORIJI. A dynamically rhythmic segment of song and dance which usually occurs at the end of a warrior play to depict battle.

DAN NO UTA (scene song). A sung segment sung usually accompanied by dance which includes mimetic action of visual interest.

DEHA MUSIC. Rhythmic entrance music usually accompanying the entrance of a non-human character in the second act. It is played by all three drums and the flute.

EI. Sung poetry with a highly inflected melody. See **genoei** and **jōnoei**.

GENOEI. A sung segment with a highly inflected melody centering on the lower register; characteristically used for the delivery of a poem. Compare **jōnoei**.

HANOMAI. A two-section instrumental dance that sometimes follows the quiet dance, usually with some text between the two dances. Despite its quick tempo, the hanomai has a flowing grace characteristic of women plays.

HAYAFUE MUSIC (fast flute music). Lively entrance music played in the second act of a first- or fifth-category play for the appearance of a vigorous god or dragon god.

IROE DANCE (color dance). A single-sequence, short instrumental dance used in the third and fourth category plays to add a moment of refined grace.

ISSEI. A song centering on the higher register that may immediately follow **issei music** or may introduce a dance. Often shared by shite and the tsure or chorus.

ISSEI MUSIC. Entrance music played by the flute and hand drums which usually announces the main character in either the first or second act.

JONOMAI (quiet dance). A slow, graceful, long instrumental dance usually done in abbreviated three-section form. It is representative of third category women plays. When the stick drum joins the ensemble, the dance is lighter; when an old woman dances, it is considerably slower.

JŌNOEI. A sung segment with a highly inflected melody centering on the higher register; characteristically used for the delivery of a poem. Compare **genoei**.

KAGURA DANCE (Shintō dance). A long instrumental dance reminiscent of Shintō ceremonies in its melody and some of its dance patterns. It is performed by priestess and goddess characters who dance with a purification wand. The stick drum always plays in the accompaniment.

KAKEAI. A dialogue segment sung in recitative style (*sashinori*). The text is usually in metered poetry. Compare **mondō**.

KAKERI (anguish dance). A two sequence action short dance to the hand drums and flute. Used in warrior and mad woman people plays to depict mental suffering.

KATARI. A relatively long, spoken, narrative segment. It may be delivered by the shite, the waki or, during the interlude, by the kyōgen.

KIRI (final). The concluding segment of a play which combines chant and dance. The dance usually has varied and active movement.

KOGAKI (variant performance). Variant renditions of noh plays incorporating adjustments in text, actions or costume to heighten a given interpretation. Special, more difficult music and dance forms add interest, and extensive use of the bridge often occurs.

KOKATA (child actor). Roles played by children. Although they often represent real children, such as the young serving girls in *Ōeyama*, they sometimes represent high ranking nobility, such as the emperor or Yoshitsune, the theory being that these people are so superior that it would be offensive to represent them realistically.

KŌKEN (stage attendants). The shite actors responsible for dressing the main actor and sitting at the rear of the stage to take care of details of performance. In the event that the main actor is incapacitated, the main stage attendant takes his part.

KURI (ornate song). A short ornate segment of poetry sung in the high register and rising to the highest pitch normally used in noh chanting (called *kuri*). The segment ends with a long embellished syllable. It is most often sung by the chorus.

KUSE. A segment central to many presentation scenes in either the first or second act of a play. The song has three sections, is largely sung by the chorus, and has strong rhythmic interest. The shite usually sings one line (*ageha*) which raises the chant to the higher register. In a double kuse (*nidanguse*) the song is expanded to five sections, and the shite sing two separated lines. The kuse may be performed with the shite seated at center stage (*iguse*) or dancing (*maiguse*).

KUSE SCENE. The scene which centers around the kuse segment and derives from a medieval performing art called *kusemai* which Kan'ami is said to have incorporated into noh. It most often consists of a **shidai, kuri, sashi,** and **kuse,** closing with a repetition of the text of the shidai.

KYŌGEN. 1) The independent, humorous plays performed between noh plays. 2) The interludes within noh plays are technically called *aikyōgen* or simply *ai*. 3) The actors who perform both 1 and 2 (*kyōgen kata*).

There are currently two schools of kyōgen actors: Izumi and Okura. The Sagi school no longer performs.

MAIBATARAKI (danced action). A two-sequence dance of vigorous tempo performed by gods, demons, beasts and ghosts in first and fifth category plays. All three drums and the flute accompany the dance. One variant version is a choreographed fight.

MICHIYUKI (travel song). Sung descriptions of travel by either the waki at the beginning of a play or by a shite or tsure (who might also dance). Usually comprise of an **ageuta** with or without a preceding **sageuta**.

MONDŌ. A spoken segment in the form of a dialogue. Often a question and answer segment between the shite and the waki.

NANORI (name announcement). A spoken segment in which a character introduces himself. Most often it is performed by the waki upon entering. It may follow a **shidai** or begin the text of the play.

NANORI MUSIC (name announcing flute). A flute solo played for the entrance of the waki in some plays in which the first sung segment is a **nanori**.

NANORIZASHI. A recitative (sashi) style name announcing segment. See **nanori**.

NIDANGUSE. See **kuse**.

NORIJI. Sung segments with a distinctive rhythmic pulse often accompanied by the stick drum. Often performed by a non-human character or used to express strong emotional states.

OMO. The designation given to the main kyōgen actor when more than one appear in the interludes of noh plays. In kyōgen play the main actor is usually called shite. Compare **ado**.

RONGI. A song segment usually shared by the shite and the chorus. It has a strong rhythm and may occur at the end of the first act where the shite's identity is revealed.

SAGEUTA. A segment of metered poetry sung in the lower register. It often precedes an **ageuta** or a **rongi** and is quite short.

SASHI (recitative). A recitative segment of unmetered poetry. Sashi segments often precede song-type (**uta**) segments and the **kuse**. Often used for lyrical monologues.

SHIDAI. 1) The first song after the shidai music. It is song by the actor(s) who enter and is usually repeated in a low voice by the chorus, though this is seldom noted in the text. 2) A shidai may be sung by the chorus as an introduction to a **kuse scene** (*jishidai*).

SHIDAI MUSIC. Quiet entrance music played by the hand drums and flute to accompany the entrance of the waki or the shite.

SHIN NO ISSEI MUSIC. Majestic entrance music for disguised deities, performed by the flute and hand drums. See **issei music**.

SHITE (main role). 1) The main role in a noh play. In two act plays the main characters in the different acts may be unrelated, but they are usually both played by the same actor. Shite actors (*shite kata*) also play tsure roles, sing in the chorus and serve as stage attendants. There are five schools of shite actors: Hshō, Kanze, Kita, Konparu and Kongō. 2) The main character in a kyōgen is also labelled shite. Compare **omo**.

SHITE SPOT. The upstage right area of the stage (called *jōza* or *nanoriza*). See stage diagram at beginning of book. The pillar in that corner of the stage, where the bridge joins the stage, is call the shite pillar (*shite bashira*).

SHŌDAN (segment). The primary units performance. Each shōdan has a characteristic form of poetry, rhythm, melody, instrumentation, and kinetics.

TSUKIZERIFU (arrival announcement). A short, spoken segment announcing arrival at a particular place. Most often used by waki and wakizure.

TSURE (companion actor). Supporting role accompanying the shite. In many plays the tsure has little action and sits for the most part in the waki seat, but in some plays the tsure role is almost equal to that of the shite. All secondary female roles are played by tsure, as waki actors never wear masks. Compare **wakizure**.

UTA (song). A segment of sung metered poetry not distinctive enough to be labelled an **ageuta** or a **sageuta**.

WAKA (poem). A sung segment the text of which is usually a classical Japanese poem (*waka*) or part of one. Sometimes a waka segment is divided into two parts to frame an instrumental dance.

WAKAUKE A segment which serves as a transition between a **waka** and a **noriji** segment.

WAKI (secondary role). 1) Usually the first actor to enter the stage in noh plays, the waki sets the scene and draws out the tale of the shite by posing questions. Many waki portray travelling priests, others are courtiers, emissaries, or other male characters. The waki never wears a mask and hence plays only living, male characters. After his entrance scene, the waki is seated at upstage left beside the **waki spot**. Waki actors, who play only waki and wakizure roles, belong to three schools: Fukuō, Hōshō and Takayasu. 2) The similar role in noh-like kyōgen. Compare **ado**.

WAKI SPOT. We have labelled the downstage left area of the stage the waki spot (usually called *wakiza mae*). See stage diagram at beginning of book. The downstage left pillar is called the waki pillar (*waki bashira*), and the waki sits for most of the play between that pillar and the chorus in a position called the *waki za*.

WAKIZURE (waki companion). Companions to the waki. Compare **tsure**.

YOBIKAKE (calling out). A spoken segment in which the shite calls out from beyond the curtain before entering the bridge.

BIBLIOGRAPHY

I. Finding list for Western language translations of plays mentioned.

Aoi no Ue: Pound 1917, Waley 1921, Steinilber-Oberlin and Matsuo 1929, Shimanouchi and Aker 1937, Zachert 1947, Nippon Gakujustu Shinkōkai II 1959, Sieffert II 1979, Goff ms

Arashiyama: Renondeau 1961

Ataka: Brinkley 1901, Sansom 1910, Nippon Gakujutsu Shinkōkai III 1960, Yasuda 1972

Atsumori: Arrivet 1895, Waley 1921 (also in Keene 1955), Péri 1944, Weber-Schafer 1961, Shimazaki 1983

Dōjōji: Sadler 1934, Keene 1970

Funa Benkei: Florenz 1906, Sansom 1910, Sidehara 1937, Nippon Gakujutsu Shinkōkai I 1955, Renondeau 1953-54

Futari Shizuka: Suzuki 1932, Shimazaki 1981, Mueller 1981

Go: Goff ms

Hanagatami: Arnold 1956, Sieffert II 1979

Hanjo: Renondeau 1961, Keene 1970

Hashibenkei: Waley 1921, Péri 1944

Hyakuman: Tyler 1978b, Sieffert 1979

Izutsu: Renondeau 1953-54, Nippon Gakujutsu Shinkōkai 1955, Arnold 1956, Weber-Schafer 1961, Shimazaki 1977, Tyler 1978b, Hare 1986

Jinen koji: Ueda 1962, Tyler 1978a

Kagetsu: none known

Kasuga ryūgin: Sieffert I 1979, Morrell 1982

Kinuta: Pound 1917, Péri 1944, Nippon Gakujutsu Shinkōkai 1960, Kato 1977, Tyler 1978b

Kurozuka: Sieffert II 1979 (as *Adachigahara*)

Matsukaze: Waley 1921, Keene 1970, Shimazaki 1977, Tyler 1978a

Motomezuka: Nippon Gakujutsu Shinkokai 1959, Keene 1970

Nishikigi Pound 1917, Keene 1970

Nue: Tyler 1978b

Rashōmon: none known

Sakuragawa: Sansom 1910, Huey 1983

Sekidera komachi: Weber-Schafer 1960, Keene 1970, Tyler 1978a

Shunkan: Parker and Morisawa 1949, Nippon Gakujutsu Shinkōkai III 1960, Sieffert II 1979

Sotoba Komachi: Waley 1921, Péri 1944, Keene 1955, Weber-Schafer 1960, Nippon Gakujutsu Shinkōkai III 1969, Tyler 1978b, Terasaki 1984

Suma Genji: Pound 1917, Weber-Schafer 1961, Goff ms

Sumidagawa: Renondeau 1950, Nippon Gakujutsu Shinkōkai I 1955, Weber-Schafer 1961

Tadanobu: none known

Tama no i: Gundert 1925, Nippon Gakujutsu Shinkōkai III 1960

Tango monogurui: Waley 1927 (summary)

Tatsuta: Gundert 1925

Tōboku: Nippon Gakujutsu Shinkōkai 1955

Tomoe: Sadler 1934, Nippon Gakujutsu Shinkōkai III 1960, Sieffert I 1979

Tsuchigumo: Suzuki 1932, Sieffert I 1979

Ukon: none known

Yamamba: Minagawa 1926, Nippon Gakujutsu Shinkōkai II 1959, Tyler 1978b

Youchi soga: Renondeau 1954, Kominz 1978

II. Works Cited

ABRAMS, M.H.
1988   *A Glossary of Literary Terms*. NY: Holt, Rinehart and Winston:
            First Edition 1957, Fifth Edition, 1988.

ARNOLD, Paul
1956   "Trois nō japonais: *Hanagatami, Hatsuyuki, Izutsu*, pour la
            première fois traduits du japonais," *Revue Théâtrale* 10, 34: 43-
            74.

ARRIVET, A.
1895   "*Atsumori*: Drame historique japonais du XVIII siècle," *Revue
            francaise du japon* 4: 479-98.

ASTON, W.G., tr.
1956   *Nihongi: Chronicles of Japan from the Earliest Times to A.D.
            697*. Supplement to The Transactions and Proceedings of the
            Japan Society, London: Kegan Paul, Trench, Truber & Co Ltd,
            1896. Reprints: London: George Allen & Unwin Ltd, 1956;
            Rutland, VT: Charles E. Tuttle Co., 1972.

BARRY, Jackson G.
1970   *Dramatic Structure: The Shaping of Experience*. Berkeley, CA:
            University of California Press.

BETHE, Monica
1984   "Nō Costume as Interpretation" and "Okina: An Interview with
            Takabayashi Koji" in *Mime Journal* 1984: *Nō/Kyōgen Masks
            and Performance*, ed. by Rebecca Teale.   Claremont CA: Po-
            mona College Theater.

BETHE, Monica and Karen BRAZELL
1978   *Nō as Performance: An Analysis of the Kuse Scene of Yamamba*.
            Cornell University East Asia Papers 16. Ithaca, NY.: China-
            Japan Program, 1978.

1982   *Dance in the Nō Theater*. Cornell University East Asia Papers
            29. Ithaca, NY.: China-Japan Program, 1982.

BLOOM, Harold
1973   *The Anxiety of Influence: A Theory of Poetry*. NY: Oxford Uni-
            versity Press.

BŌSHIBARI (translation of)
1882   "Pinioned" *The Chrysanthemum* 2,8: 353-361.

BRAZELL, Karen
1980   "Blossoms': A Medieval Song," *Journal of Japanese Studies* 6,
            2: 243-266.

1981   "Unity of Image: An Aspect of the Art of Noh," *Japanese Tradi-
            tion: Search and Research*: Los Angeles: University of Califor-
            nia, Asian Performing Arts Summer Institute.

1982-83   *"Atsumori*: The Ghost of a Warrior on Stage," *Par Rapport* 5-6
            (1982-83): 13-23.

BRINKLEY, F.
1901   *Japan, Its History, Arts and Literature*. Boston and Tokyo: J.B.
            Millet Co.

BROWER, Robert, and Earl MINER
1961   Japanese Court Poetry. Stanford, CA: Stanford University
            Press.

BURCH, NOEL
1979   *To the Distant Observer: Form and meaning in the Japanese Cin-
            ema*. Berkeley and Los Angeles, University of California.

FURUKAWA Hisashi, ed.
1964-66   Kyōgenshu, 3 vols. Nihon koten zensho 43-45. Tokyo: Asahi
            shinbunsha, 1964-66.

GOFF, Janet
1982   *"The Tale of Genji* as a Source of the Nō: *Yūgao* and *Hajitomi*,"
            Harvard Journal of Asiatic Studies 42 (June 1982): 177-229.

1984   "The New National Noh Theatre," *Monumenta Nipponica* 39,4
            (Winter 1984): 445-52.

Ms   *The Tale of Genji* as a Source of the Noh.

GUNDERT, Wilhelm
1925   "Der Schintoismus im japanischen No-Drama," *Mitteilungen
            der deutschen Gessellschaft für Natur und Volkerkunde Ostasiens*
            19.

HARE, Thomas Blenman
1986   *Zeami's Style: The Noh Plays of Zeami Motokiyo*. Stanford, CA:
            Stanford University Press.

HASHIMOTO Asao
1984   "Chūsei kyōgenshi nenpyō," *Nōgaku kenkyū* 10 (1984): 109-41.

HAYNES, Carolyn
1984   "Parody in *Kyōgen: Makura monogurui* and *Tako*," *Monumenta Nipponica* 39 (1984):

1988   *Parody in the Maikyōgen and the Monogurui Kyōgen*. Ph.D. dissertation. Cornell University, January 1988.

1988   "Comic Inversion in Kyōgen: Ghosts and the Nether World," *Journal of Association of Teachers of Japanese*, in press.

HERNADI, Paul
1972   *Beyond Genre: New Directions in Literary Classification*. Ithaca, NY: Cornell University Press.

HOFF, Frank and Willi FLINT
1973   "The Life Structure of Noh," (adapted from the Japanese of Yokomichi Mario), *Concerned Theatre Japan* 2 (Spring 1973): 209-256.

HUEY, Robert N., tr.
1983   *"Sakuragawa*: Cherry River." *Monumenta Nipponica* 38, 3 (Autumn 1983): 295-312.

HURVITZ, Leon, tr.
1976   *Scripture of the Lotus Blossom of the Fine Dharma*. NY: Columbia University Press.

IKEDA Hiroshi and KITAHARA Yasuo, eds.
1972-83   *Ōkura Toraakirabon: Kyōgenshū no kenkyū*, 3 vols. Tokyo: Hyōgensha.

INAGAKI Hisao with P.G. O'NEILL
1984   *A Dictionary of Japanese Buddhist Terms* (Based on References in Japanese Literature). Kyoto: Nagata bunshodo.

ITŌ Masayoshi, ed.
1983-86   *Yōkyokūshu*. 2 volumes. Shinchō Nihon koten shūsei. Tokyo: Shinchōsha, 1983, 1986. (A third volume is planned.)

IZUTSU Toshiko and Toyo IZUTSU
1981   *The Theory of Beauty in the Classical Aesthetics of Japan*. The Hague: Martinus Nijhoff.

KAKEI Iori
1929   "Hyakuren shokai no kenkyu" in *Kokugo to kokubungaku* 6, 1 (January 1929): 95-130.

KANZE Sakon, the 24th
1980   *Miwa*. Kanzeryū utaibon. Tokyo: Hinoki shoten.

KATAGIRI Yōichi
1969   *Ise monogatari no kenkyū (shiryōhen)*. Tokyo: Meiji shoin, 1969.

KATŌ, Eileen, tr.
1977   "Kinuta." *Monumenta Nipponica* 32, 3 (Autumn 1977): 332-346.

KAWAGUCHI Hisao and SHIDA Nobuyoshi, eds.
1965   *Wakan rōeishū Ryojin hishō*. Nihon koten bungaku taikei 73. Tokyo: Iwanami shoten, 1965.

KEENE, Donald
1955   *Anthology of Japanese Literature*. New York: Grove Press.

1966   *No: The Classical Theater of Japan*. Tokyo: Kodansha International.

1970   *Twenty Plays of the Nō Theatre*. New York: Columbia University Press.

KENNY, Don
1989   *The Kyogen Book: An Anthology of Japanese Classical Comedies*. Tokyo: The Japan Times.

KIDŌ Saizō and SHIGEMATSU Hiromi, eds.
1972   *Chūsei no bungaku*, Renga ronshū 1, first series. Tokyo: Miyai shoten.

KOKURITSU NŌGAKUDŌ
1987   *Kokuritsu nōgakudō*, 49 (September, 1987).

KOMINZ, Lawrence
1978   "The Noh as Popular Theater: Miyamasu's *Youchi Soga*," *Monumenta Nipponica* 33: 441-459.

KOMPARU Kunio
1983   *The Noh Theater: Principles and perspectives*. New York, Tokyo, Kyoto: Weatherhill/Tankosha.

KONISHI Jin'ichi
1958   "Association and Progression: Principles of Integration in Anthologies and Sequences of Japanese Court Poetry, A.D. 900-1350," translated and adapted by Earl Miner and Robert H. Brower, *Harvard Journal of Asiatic Studies*, 21 (1958): 67-127.

1960   "New Approaches to the study of the Nō Drama," *Tokyō kyōiku daigaku bungakubu kiyō*, 5 (1960): 1-31.

1972   "Sakuhin kenkyū: *Genji kuyō*," *Kanze* (April 1972).

1985   "Michi and Medieval Writing" in *Principles of Japanese Literature*, ed. by Earl Miner. Princeton, NJ: Princeton University Press.

KOYAMA Hiroshi, ed.
1960-61   *Kyōgenshū*, 2 vols. Nihon koten bungaku taikei 42-43. Tokyo: Iwanami shoten.

KOYAMA Hiroshi, et. al., eds.
1973-75   *Yokyōkushū* 2 vols. Nihon koten bungaku zenshū 33, 34. Tokyo: Shōgakkan, 1973, 1975.

MCCULLOUGH, Helen Craig, tr.
1966   *Yoshitsune: A Fifteenth-Century Japanese Chronicle*. Stanford, CA: Stanford University Press.

1968   *Tales of Ise: Lyrical Episodes from Tenth-Century Japan*. Stanford, CA: Stanford University Press.

1985a   *Kokin Wakashu: The First Imperial Anthology of Japanese Poetry*. Stanford, CA: Stanford University Press.

1985b   *Brocade by Night: Kokin Wakashu and the Court Style in Japanese Classical Poetry*. Stanford, CA: Stanford University Press.

1988   *The Tale of the Heike*. Stanford, CA: Stanford University Press.

MCKINNON, Richard N.
1968   *Selected Plays of Kyōgen*. Tokyo: Uniprint Inc.

MINAGAWA, M.
1926   "*Yamauba*," *The Young East* 2: 85-93.

MINER, Earl, Hiroko ODAGIRI and Robert E. MORRELL
1985   *The Princeton Companion to Classical Japanese Literature*. Princeton, New Jersey: Princeton University Press.

MOI, Toril, ed.
1986   *The Kristeva Reader*. NY: Columbia University Press.

MORIMOTO Shigeru
1969   *Ise monogatari ron*. Tokyo: Daigakudo shoten.

MORRELL, Robert E. tr.
1982   "Passage to India Denied: Zeami's *Kasuga ryūjin*," *Monumenta Nipponica* 37: 190-200.

MORSON, Gary Saul
1981   *The Boundaries of Genre: Dostoevsky's Diary of a Writer and the Traditions of Literary Utopia.* Austin: University of Texas Press.

MUELLER, Jacqueline
1981   "The Two Shizukas. Zeami's *Futari Shizuka.*" *Monumenta Nipponica*, 36, 3 (Autumn 1981): 285-298.

MURASAKI Shikibu
1976   *The Tale of Genji.* Translated by Edward G. Seidensticker. NY: Alfred A. Knopf.

NEARMAN, Mark, tr.
1978   "Zeami's *Kyu'i:* A Pedagogical Guide for 'Teachers of Acting," *Monumenta Nipponica* 33,3 (Autumn 1978): 299-332.

1980   *Kyakuraika,* Zeami's Final Legacy for the Master Actor," *Monumenta Nipponica* 25,2 (Summer 1980) 153-97.

1982-83   "*Kakyō,*" 3 parts, *Monumenta Nipponica* 37,3 (autumn 1982): 233-74; 37,4 (Winter 1982): 461-96; 38,1 (Spring 1983): 51-71.

NIPPON GAKUJUTSU SHINKOKAI, tr.
1955-60   *Japanese Noh Drama.* 3 vols. Tokyo: Nippon gakujutsu shinkōkai, 1955, 1959, 1960. Volume I reprinted as *The Noh Drama.* Tokyo and Rutland, Vermont: Tuttle, 1973.

NOGAMI Toyōichiro
1971   *(Kaichū) Yōkyoku zenshū,* 6 vols. Tokyo: Chūōkoronsha, first edition 1949-51. Reprint 1971.

NONOMURA Kaizō
1935   Kyōgen buyōshū. Tokyo: Tōkyokukai shuppanbu.

NONOMURA Kaizō and ANDŌ Tsunejirō, eds.
1974   *Kyōgen shūsei.* Tokyo: Shun'yōdō, 1931. Expanded and revised edition, Nōgaku shorin, 1974.

OKAMI Masao, ed.
1959   *Gikeiki.* Nihon koten bungaku taikei 37. Tokyo: Iwanami shoten.

OMOTE Akira and KATŌ Shūichi
1974   *Zeami Zenchiku.* Nihon shisō taikei 24. Tokyo: Iwanami shoten.

O'NEILL, P.G.
1974   *Early Nō Drama: Its Background, Character and Development 1330-1450.* First edition 1958. Reprint, Westport, Connecticut: Greenwood, 1974.

PARKER, C.K. and S. MORISAWA trs.
1949 "Shunkan," *Monumenta Nipponica* 4: 246-55.

PÉRI, Noël, tr.
1944 Le nō. Tokio: Maison franco-japonaise.

PHILIPPI, Donald L., tr.
1969 *Kojiki*. Princeton, NJ: Princeton University Press.

POLLACK, David
1986 *The Fracture of Meaning: Japan's Synthesis of China from the Eighth through the Eighteenth Centuries*. Princeton N.J.: Princeton University Press.

POUND, Ezra and Ernest FENOLLOSA, tr.
1959 *The Classical Noh Theatre of Japan*. First edition, 1917; reprint, New York: New Directions, 1959.

RENONDEAU, Gaston, tr.

1950 *Le Bouddhisme dans les nō*. Tokyo: Maison Franco-Japonaise.

1953-54 *Nō*, 2 vols. Tokyo: Maison Franco-japonaise.

1961 "Cinq Nō I: Arashi-yama," *France-Asia* 17: 1889-1908, "IV: Hanjo": 2781-2794.

1963 "Trois Kyōgen: Bōshibari," *France-Asie* 19 (October-December, 1963): 1005-1011.

RIMER, J. Thomas and Masakazu YAMAZAKI, tr.
1984 *On the Art of the Nō Drama: The Major Treatises of Zeami*. Princeton: Princeton University Press.

SADLER, Arthur Lindsay, tr.
1934 *Japanese Plays: Nō Kyōgen Kabuki*. Sydney: Angus.

SANSOM, George
1910 "Translations from the Nō," *Translations of the Asiatic Society of Japan* 38: 133-176.

SANARI Kentarō, ed.

1930-31 *Yōkyoku taikan*, 7 vols. Tokyo: Meiji shoin, 1931-33. Reprints 1964, 1982.

SCHMIED, Wieland, tr.
1963 "'Kakitsubata' (Die Zeitlose) von Seami Motokiyo," *Merkur* 17 (May 1963): 446-53.

SHIMANOUCHI Toshiro and William AKER
1937   *The Noh Drama.* Tokyo: Kokusai bunka shinkokai.

SHIMAZAKI Chifumi, tr.
1972-83   *The Noh*, 5 vols. Tokyo: Hinoki shoten, 1972, 1976, 1977, 1981,
            1983.

SIDEHARA Michitarō
1937   *Funa-Benkei.* Tokyo: Kokusai Bunka Shinkōkai.

SIEFFERT, René
1960   *La Tradition sécrète du Nō.* Paris: Gallimard, 1960.

1979   *Nō et Kyōgen: Théatre du Moyen Age*, 2 vols. Paris: Publica-
            tions Orientalistes de France.

STEINILBER-OBERLIN, Émile and Kuni MATSUO
1929   *Le livre de nō, drames légendaires du vieux japon.* Paris:
            H.Piazza, 1929.

SUZUKI, Beatrice Lane, tr.
1932   *Nōgaku, Japanese Nō Plays.* New York.

TAKAGI Ichinosuke, et. al., eds.
1969   *Heike monogatari*, Book II. Nihon koten bungaku taikei, 33.
            Tokyo: Iwanami shoten.

TANAKA Makoto, ed.
1957   *Yōkyokushū*, 3 vols. Nihon koten zenshū. Tokyo: Asahi sh-
            inbunsha.

TERASAKI Etsuko
1978   "The Representation of Reality in the Nō Theatre: *Hachi no
            ki*," *Journal of the Association of Teachers of Japanese* 13,2.

1984   "Images and Symbols in *Sotoba Komachi*: A Critical Analysis of
            a Nō Play," *Harvard Journal of Asiatic Studies* 44, 1.

1988   "Wild Words and Specious Phrases: *Kyōgen/kigo* in the Nō Play
            Jinen koji," *Harvard Journal of Asiatic Studies*, in press.

TOITA Michizō
1984   *Nō no jiten.* Tokyo: Sanseidō.

TOMIKURA Tokujirō, ed.
1968   *Heike monogatari zen chūshaku.* Tokyo: Kadokawa shoten.

TYLER, Royall, tr.
1978a   *Pining Wind: A Cycle of Nō Plays.* East Asia Papers 17. Ithaca,
            New York: China-Japan Program.

1978b   *Granny Mountains: A Second Cycle of No Plays*. East Asia Papers 18. Ithaca, New York: China-Japan Program.

UEDA Makoto tr.
1962   *The Old Pine and Other Noh Plays*. Lincoln, Nebraska; University of Nebraska Press.

VOS, Frits
1957   *A Study of the Ise-Monogatari*, 2 vols. The Hague: Mouton & Co.

WALEY, Arthur, tr.
1921   *The Nō Plays of Japan*. London: Allen and Unwin, 1921. Reprint NY: Grove Press, 1957.

WATSON, Burton, tr.
1984   *The Columbia Book of Chinese Poetry*. NY: Columbia University Press.

WEBER-SCHAFER, Peter, tr.
1960   *Ono no Komachi: Gestalt und Legende in Nō-Spiel*. Wiesbaden: Otto Harrassowitz.

1961   *Vierundzwandig No-Spiele*. Frankfurt a.M.: Insel-Verlag.

YAMAGISHI Tokuhei, ed.
1958   *Genji monogatari*, book 1. Nihon koten bungaku taikei 14. Tokyo: Iwanami shoten.

YASUDA, Kenneth
1972   "The Dramatic Structure of *Ataka*," *Monumenta Nipponica* 27: 359-98.

YOKOMICHI Mario and OMOTE Akira, eds.
1960-63   *Yōkyokushū*, 2 vols. Nihon koten bungaku taikei 40, 41. Tokyo: Iwanami shoten, 1960, 1963.

YOSHIDA Kōichi, ed.
1953-62   *Izūmiryu kyōgenshū*, 20 vols. Tokyo: Koten bunko.

ZACHERT, Herbert, tr.
1947   "*Aoi no Ue*. Nō-Drama in zwei Akten von Komparu Ujinobu,"

CORNELL EAST ASIA SERIES

For ordering information, please contact:

Cornell East Asia Series
East Asia Program
Cornell University
140 Uris Hall
Ithaca, NY 14853-7601
USA
(607) 255-6222.

1-93/.6M/BB

Printed in the USA
CPSIA information can be obtained
at www.ICGtesting.com
LVHW051140011223
765185LV00002B/194